THE DEPTH OF HER SOUL

BEAUTIFUL STORIES OF FAITH AND EMPOWERMENT

Compiled by: Monica Kunzekweguta

LWL PUBLISHING HOUSE

Brampton, Canada

The Depth of Her Soul – Beautiful Stories of Faith and Empowerment

Copyright © 2016 by LWL PUBLISHING HOUSE
A division of Anita Sechesky – Living Without Limitations Inc.

All rights reserved. No part of this publication may be reproduced, distributed or transmitted in any form or by any means, including photocopying, recording, or other electronic or mechanical methods, without prior written permission of the publisher, except in the case of brief quotations embodied in critical reviews and certain other noncommercial uses permitted by copyright law. For permission requests, write to the publisher, addressed "Attention: Permissions Coordinator," at the address below.

Anita Sechesky – Living Without Limitations Inc.
asechesky@hotmail.ca
lwlclienthelp@gmail.com
www.lwlpublishinghouse.com

Publisher's Note: This book is a collection of personal experiences written at the discretion of each contributor. LWL PUBLISHING HOUSE uses American English spelling as its standard. Each co-author's word usage and sentence structure have remained unaltered as much as possible to retain the authenticity of each chapter.

Book Layout © 2016 LWL PUBLISHING HOUSE

The Depth of Her Soul – Beautiful Stories of Faith and Empowerment
Anita Sechesky – Living Without Limitations Inc.
ISBN 978-0-9939648-1-7
ASIN 0993964817

Book Cover: LWL PUBLISHING HOUSE
Inside Layout: LWL PUBLISHING HOUSE

CONTENTS

LEGAL DISCLAIMER _____ 1

FOREWORD _____ 3

ACKNOWLEDGEMENTS _____ 5

INTRODUCTION _____ 7

CHAPTER 1 _____ 13
The Masked Power in Words
Monica Kunzekweguta

CHAPTER 2 _____ 19
Appreciating My Homeland Heritage
Tracy Kadungure

CHAPTER 3 _____ 25
The Bond between Mother and Child
Zothile Tatenda

CHAPTER 4 _____ 31
Courage to Heal - Lessons from My Mother
Joy Mutare

CHAPTER 5 _____ 37
Abused, but Not a Victim
Ruvarashe Ruzive

CHAPTER 6 _____ 43
My Strength Comes From Within
Melody Mbondiah

CHAPTER 7 _____ 49
A Season of Faith's Perfection
Andrée Nicole

CHAPTER 8 _____ 55
Circumstances Cannot Determine One's Future
Jonathan Zhungu

CHAPTER 9 _____ 63
My Precious Hand Bag
Margareth Nyakambangwe

CHAPTER 10 _____ 69
Little Girl, Grown
Debra Mowlem

CHAPTER 11 _____ 75
Is Being Single a Curse?
Jossine Kaizirwe

CHAPTER 12 _____ 81
Back from Hell and Still Smelling like Roses!
Faith Ekperuoh

CHAPTER 13 _____ 87
Removing Toxins from Your Life, Even Those Walking on Two Legs
Dora Arabou

CHAPTER 14 _____ 93
I Overcame Being My Worst Enemy
Dorcas Marimo

CHAPTER 15 _____ 99
Her Labor of Love
Langton Wilsey Chibuwe

CHAPTER 16 _____ 105
Restoration of Hope
Lynette Mutasa

CHAPTER 17 _____ 111
My Journey so Far
Sibinah Adewole

CHAPTER 18 _____ 117
Breaking the Bullying Cycle
Monica Kunzekweguta

CHAPTER 19 _____ 123
A Woman Empowered
Emily Mapfuwa

CHAPTER 20 _____ 129
A Mother's Love
Godknows Kudzanayi Mashaire

CHAPTER 21 _____ 135
All about Me!
Sikumbuzo Thabethe

CHAPTER 22 _____ 141
A Woman's Beauty is the Depth of Her Soul
Harold Sharara

CHAPTER 23 _____ 147
God-given Opportunities
Thobekile Mutezo

CHAPTER 24 _____ 153
Stand By Me
Crystal Cathell

CHAPTER 25 _____ 159
Walking Through Fire
Leah Lucas

CONCLUSION _____ 167

LEGAL DISCLAIMER

The information and content contained within this book *The Depth of Her Soul – Beautiful Stories of Faith and Empowerment* does not substitute any form of professional counsel such as a Psychologist, Physician, Life Coach, or Counselor. The contents and information provided does not constitute professional or legal advice in any way, shape or form.

All chapters are written at the discretion of and with the full accountability of each writer. Anita Sechesky – Living Without Limitations Inc. or LWL PUBLISHING HOUSE is not liable or responsible for any of the specific details, descriptions of people, places or things, personal interpretations, stories and experiences contained within. The Publisher is not liable for any misrepresentations, false or unknown statements, actions, or judgements made by any of the contributors or their chapter contents in this book. Each contributor is responsible for their own submissions and have shared their stories in good faith to encourage others.

Any decisions you make and the outcomes thereof are entirely your own doing. Under no circumstances can you hold the Compiler, LWL PUBLISHING HOUSE, or "Anita Sechesky – Living Without Limitations Inc." liable for any actions that you take.
You agree not to hold the Compiler, LWL PUBLISHING HOUSE, or "Anita Sechesky – Living Without Limitations Inc." liable for any loss or expense incurred by you, as a result of materials, advice, coaching or mentoring offered within.
The information offered in this book is intended to be general information with respect to general life issues. Information is offered in good faith; however you are under no obligation to use this information.

Nothing contained in this book shall be considered legal, financial, or actuarial advice.

The author or Publisher assume no liability or responsibility to actual events or stories being portrayed.

It may introduce what a Life Coach, Counselor or Therapist may discuss with you at any given time during scheduled sessions. The advice contained herein is not meant to replace the Professional roles of a physician or any of these professions.

FOREWORD

It brings me great joy to publish this book that my friend and colleague, Monica Kunzekweguta has compiled. She has successfully co-authored in four of my Best-Selling anthologies to date. Therefore, working alongside her to birth this anthology has been a great pleasure to experience. I have witnessed the challenges she has endured to bring her vision for this book to life, and I'm so grateful that she never gave up when it could have been so easy, or expected, for her to do so.

Life holds no guarantees, nor are promises always fulfilled. The vision for *The Depth of Her Soul – Beautiful Stories of Faith and Empowerment* was a labor of love for Monica to create, as it was for each valuable contributor who stood by her side. Although the growing pains were ever-present, never did I hear Monica complain or say that she was ready to quit. As I reviewed the chapters that were submitted, and learned about the struggles and hardships many of the co-authors endured, I saw one common theme emerging time and time again – perseverance and courage, coupled with a good dose of faith and inspiration, lavishly sprinkled throughout each one of the chapters. These are the kinds of stories that I'm so proud to be publishing. To me, this is what "Living Without Limitations" is all about: to encourage, as well as bring hope and healing to all those who resonate with these messages.

When you read this book, you will be exposed to various types of crises, trauma, and persecution. You will understand the doubts, insecurities, rejection, and fears these writers have lived through. Your perspectives will be enlightened to appreciate that, although things may seem difficult at the moment, it does not have to be that way forever. The amazing thing about these stories is that each contributor has come out stronger and have never allowed their hardships and negative experiences to diminish their "soul purpose" during their journeys. Instead, they chose to find the joy, love, and peace that life still has to offer.

As an individual who has gone through my own painful experiences, and decided to forgive and move forward in faith and expectancy, I celebrate the unconditional love that Monica and her beautiful co-authors have shared with the world. Thank you Monica and team.

"For beauty is not skin deep, but it is deep within a person's soul."

Anita Sechesky

Anita is a Best-Seller Publisher, Registered Nurse, Certified Professional Coach, NLP and LOA Wealth Practitioner, Media Marketing Mentor, International Best-Selling Author, as well as Workshop Facilitator and Conference Host. She is the Founder and CEO of Anita Sechesky - Living Without Limitations Inc. and the Founder and Publisher of LWL PUBLISHING HOUSE. Anita was born in Guyana, South America and moved to Canada when she was four years old. She has assisted many people breaking through their own limiting beliefs in life and business.

Anita has six Best-Selling anthologies to date, three of which her company has published as well as two client compilations, and has two more anthologies to be released in 2016. Anita has worked with, mentored, and promoted 183 International authors, out of which her company has now published 142 of these authors. Anita launched her first solo book *"Absolutely You – Overcome False Limitations and Reach Your Full Potential"* in November 2014. Currently, Anita's company has several VIP client anthologies in the works with limited co-authoring opportunities available. As a Best-Seller Publisher, Anita helps people to put their positive perspectives into print. No writing experience required.

Email: lwlclienthelp@gmail.com

www.lwlpublishinghouse.com

ACKNOWLEDGEMENTS

To my wonderful co-authors, I would like to thank you for trusting and believing in me. You shared your very private and personal stories, probably reopening wounds which were healed for the sake of helping and encouraging others. I hope this will bring a complete healing to you, through knowing that your stories will encourage someone to do something about their situation. For this reason, they will be able to change their ways or have a different perspective about life. With the utmost appreciation from the bottom of my heart, I extended my sincere gratitude to you for agreeing to work with me. Through your acceptance for us to work together, we are bound by this book project. Without your support, love, and commitment I would not have had the opportunity to compile such a powerful masterpiece, and for that I am truly grateful.

To my Publisher and mentor Anita Sechesky, you have been an amazing sister and friend. Your commitment to see everyone succeed is phenomenal. May God continue to bless you. You sacrifice a lot of family time to ensure that we are all supported on our various journeys. You are a rare gem.

To my father, I would like to take this opportunity to acknowledge you. Thank you for instilling in me the strong values which help me stay balanced and grounded in my day-to-day life. Tete Grace, your lessons will always be appreciated.

To my mum, I appreciate you. You have taught me so much about hard work and determination.

To my uncles, William, Mathew, David, Freddy, and Walter (gone but never forgotten), I love you all so much. You have always been my supporters and my advocates. It is because of your dedication to my education that I am the woman I am today. You take your role of fatherhood seriously, and I am blessed to have you in my life.

INTRODUCTION

The Depth Of Her Soul – Beautiful Stories of Faith and Empowerment is a compilation of candid and real stories aimed at both men and women celebrating the contribution of women to society and to mankind. A woman is a member of the gentler sex, who transitions from being a girl child to take various roles of sister, mother, grandmother, and eventually an elderly lady. Through her life time, she also becomes a friend, a trainer, a teacher, a mentor, and a leader. Determination, resilience, focus, healing, and love are some of the human aspects highlighted in the stories shared in this book to encourage people from all walks of life, and from around the globe, to accept challenges as a part of our journey in life. Indeed, it is true that the human spirit can ignite the power within us to become who, and what, we want to be. Male authors acknowledge how the women in their lives are instrumental in shaping them into the wonderful human beings they are today. At the same time, women share how they have used their unlimited potential, self-value, or individuality to excel in their respective journeys.

A woman is expected to cope and manage because she is the one who holds the fabric of society together. She is giving of herself most of the time, and usually forgets about her own needs completely. She understands that true beauty is first inward. Her real strength is found in being gracious, thoughtful, kind, intelligent, and self-assuredness. This can only be an act of something deeper, something not tangible, and something spiritual, which is her soul.

A woman's beauty is not in her external features, but her true beauty is in her heart.

The beauty of a woman is not determined by man. Her beauty can be found in her grace, and not just in the beauty of her face. It can be found in her style and originate in her smile. A woman's beauty is in her thoughts, not just what she has been taught, but sometimes it is found in her soul as well. It cannot go untold; her beauty is within herself. She does not need to lure anyone because of her presence; it's in her essence.

On behalf of the great team of co-authors who have made this book a success, and indeed on my own behalf, I extend our sincere gratitude to all the readers of this anthology.

The vision of the principal author is that this book will motivate and inspire women of all ages. Young and old alike constantly require this motivation and inspiration, to excel in every area of their lives. It is intended that by reading the collection of works here, women will be supported in focusing on the beauty of unlimited potential, individuality, and their own personal values. At the same time, the male audiences will be equipped with knowledge of how to channel the success of their female counterparts; whether it is a daughter, a sister, a mother, and any other relationship or friend.

This masterpiece collection of amazing and true life stories is written straight from the hearts and souls of sisters and brothers from around the world. I believe that each one of them has a special message that should be heard by many who are waiting for it.

While the vision is certain to effectively impact women of all ages, it is most significantly intended to motivate the younger ones who have so much potential within themselves, to still create the life they desire. The reader, it is hoped, will walk away with what they really want out of life; and will actively go out of their ways to find connection between their passion and their career choices.

This book will encourage and inspire the broken spirits, damaged souls, and discouraged individuals who feel that life has forgotten them. To all those who feel that they are stuck in a role they never intended, these stories are also meant to give you a nudge out of such a predicament. Among the principal author's intentions, was to also meet the need for women to understand the connection between their passion and career choices. Some of the stories in this collection are aimed at being a catalyst to soften the hearts of those that have been hardened, and to confirm that a woman's beauty is not in her physical appearance. It is in the confidence within her heart that confirms her wisdom, knowledge, and life skills that are highly valuable and sought after qualities.

The visionary's commitment is to help readers realize the beauty within and understand that they are complete; they just need to tap into the very same source, the one that has given them their talent to live a purposeful life. When we understand what is predestined for us, and are aligned with our co-values, there is no internal conflict. This disrupts the peace, love, and grace which all yearn for. It is this inner conflict which often makes some people focus on their external beauty. When one is in that space, there is no room for hate or causing harm to another. We are all connected from source and our purpose is to serve one another.

What makes this compilation a handbook for every person is that, while it's about a woman's beauty, a lot of men's contributions have left me intrigued. In particular, I have observed that most reasonable men appreciate a woman who is confident, successful, and independent. I understood that my worth and beauty as a woman was largely influenced by a special man in my life too. Growing up, my father always made me feel special, and encouraged me to be the best that I could be. It is very true that the iconic figure in a woman's life can sometimes make or break the woman's perception of self-worth. A lot of women have been downtrodden by their male counterparts, and have felt unworthy, therefore losing confidence, and hence failed to see the inner beauty that they are naturally endowed with. There is a common saying that has been used over the years, the opposite of which is also true: *Behind every successful woman is a great man.*

All readers, regardless of gender, will benefit through experiencing the personal, sometimes painful journeys that some women have had to travel.

At the end of the day, men are better off when their women expose that inner beauty from the soul. If this book helps a man to understand the benefit of assisting a woman to expose her inner beauty, then the purpose of this book would have been served. Likewise if a woman is inspired to do that of her own accord, then again the purpose is served. Ultimately the world will benefit with women who do not feel controlled, ashamed, and are hurting, but whose beauty comes from the depth of their souls!

Compiled by Monica Kunzekweguta 11

Unlimited Potential

CHAPTER 1   Monica Kunzekweguta

The Masked Power in Words

The Venetian rulers in the 16th century masqueraded with masks that hid their true faces behind them. For them, it was a strategy for royalty to disguise their power and authority during festivals so that they could mingle and indulge in pleasure. The same can be said about words – they mask the power behind them. We have been told over and over again that words are powerful. However, unless they are verbally expressed, they have no power. There are some words that talk victory, and these are contemporary like, "Yes we can!" And yet again, we have words such as "Mein Kampf" – words which led to genocide.

A lot of people have been affected and discouraged by what has been said to them, or about them. It is easy to understand why. However, what is even more serious and important are the words people speak to themselves, to their children, friends, or their students. Words have the power to destroy or build. Every civilization has taught that life and death are in the power of the tongue, and those who have loved the exercise, the bad words have always lived to fulfil this wisdom.

I was going through a social platform, and one post caught my attention. It read, "Write the saddest story you can, use only four words." I noted that within one hour, it had attracted over three hundred comments. Ninety percent of those comments were very negative and painful words to read, a few were funny and hilarious, and it made me think that was someone attempting to bring some comic relief to this grim post. At first I thought there is no way I would read such comments, then I thought, "Wait a minute, this could be so powerful if the group members were supported at the end of this painful and uncomfortable exercise." Such strong painful emotions were just being stirred up. I could feel it happening within me, but I decided not to be consumed by it. No doubt, this being an international platform, participants were commenting from all over the world. Some were writing about issues in their lives. I could not help but sense that some of these stories were current as the authors wrote them. They were actually in the middle of a crisis. Possibly a break up, a loss, or simply in total despair. These comments caught my attention; "You do not matter"; "That night meant nothing"; "Life left me slowly"; "I found a lump"; "You hurt my soul"; "And then he left"; "I trusted and fell"; "She betrayed herself again". All these statements left someone broken, and destroyed. Can you see how these four words spelt catastrophe in those people's lives? I only picked a few "stories" from that thread in order to show how deeply people were affected by words which were spoken to them. Some of them were uttered many years ago, but might still have a deep and negative impact on the writer's life. Equally positive words will go a long way in building someone up.

When I started to read, I felt my heart sink, and then I decided to ponder a little bit on it. I realized that when I wrote my very first published story, I had gone through a lot of pain and fear. The pain of reliving a sad part of my life and fear of being vulnerable, allowing the mask to come off. I was also worried about disappointing those who were part of my narrative. I remembered how writing it was a helpful and useful exercise. The result for me was very surprising; not only did I manage to heal emotionally, but it healed the broken relationship I had with my father. It also opened doors for me, and my career started to take off. It is amazing how miracles happen when you forgive yourself and others.

As I continued to read, I was taken to a discussion I had with a friend a few days earlier. She had expressed that she wanted to write a story about her life and what she had gone through. She was aware that it would help others, but most importantly help her to heal. She was not willing, however, to revisit that part of her life which was painful and filled with sadness. "I would rather leave it buried," she said. This is the same principle used in a counseling process. The counselor usually takes you back to that darkest period, and then walks you through the healing process. Sometimes we need to understand what went wrong in order to get unstuck, so that we are able to move forward with our lives.

My parents divorced in the seventies, when I was three years old. In those days, divorces were not as prevalent as they are now. At the time, children like me faced a lot of discrimination because of our circumstances. Society made us, or certainly made me, feel like there was something terribly wrong with ourselves. People would talk about my parents as if they knew their story. There was a whole host of things I was "meant" to become. People had an opinion as soon as they got to know my back ground or my circumstances. If one's situation was not what was socially "acceptable", they would be automatically ruled out, excluded from consideration for success, a good job, and in some cases interested suitors would be discouraged from marrying girls from "broken homes".

Parents, single women, divorced men and women are all made to feel a certain way. They are either made to feel incomplete or inadequate because life happens and they find themselves where they are right now. This happens at job interviews, in churches, and even with consideration for a promotion. They may be qualified and are the best candidate, but may not be chosen because of their marital status. They already have the burden of feeling that they failed their kids and family, and they do not need every sector in society judging them as well.

We have the power to face the challenges from a powerful standpoint. We cannot change how people think, but we can show them that we are here to live our lives and not apologize to anyone for doing that. Depending on how many words our lives are written in, we can always determine our own vocabulary. It is when people want to change the script that they decide not to use words that are chosen for them. Experience shows that there are those among us who choose to ask themselves the four following questions: Who am I? What do I want? What do I stand for? What do I want to be remembered for? These are questions we all struggle with. I have asked these questions myself when words were said to me. Ultimately, there is logic in establishing identity; taking action on these four questions is the quest for an individual.

You should not put any limitations on what you want. When you prepare for growth, you cannot be with the same crowd or maintain the same habits. You set your own standards and watch a beautiful story unfold. When I was young, in the 1970's, there was a general notion that children from divorced parents never amounted to anything. So many words were being thrown at me – words which were used to describe who I was, or what I would become. They said she would not finish college, have a baby before she finishes school, become a prostitute, be a failure, be poor and live a miserable life, and more. I was not even interested in having a boyfriend; at that young age, it was not my focus. I guess that is what the enemy wished for me. Judging by these words, my life had already been mapped out. No one saw a bright future. To them it was all gloom and doom. But I did not allow myself to be consumed by such negativity. In fact, I never pictured myself in any of the scenarios at all. That was not what I wanted, and it was not going to happen.

I refused to allow those words to define me. Not only did close relatives use them, but even neighbors. How many of us have replayed a negative comment passed by a stranger over and over again in our minds, allowing it to distract us from a task at hand? Or shake the strong foundation on which we stand?

Determination to have a better life is what pushed me and kept me on track. I decided that it was my journey and I was in charge of this ship. Instead of focusing on those negative definitions, I used them to remind me of who I was not, and who I would never be. Each time I thought about one of them, I would pick up my books and study. One comment from a neighbor which drove me to work hard was, "You are so lazy, let us see how you will survive if you happen to marry in this village?" The village had an irrigation system which meant that working the fields happened throughout the year. That is not how I wanted my life to go. I wanted to leave the village and live in the city. I wanted to live my life on my own terms. I was only eleven years old and already had decided that I was not going to let anything or anyone define me. This was just a neighbor who for some reason felt it was okay to destroy someone else's child, just by using words. My tenacity and resilience paid off. I passed and ended up graduating with a degree in Sociology, worked in management positions for many years, and now I am an author and a speaker. My passion is to speak life into people's dreams and help them discard the bad seeds which were planted in their soil. Their soil is good soil, but the seeds planted in them are ruined and will not germinate and produce good fruits. I am pleased to say that it was not all bad. I had people who believed in me so much, their words were a good reminder that I was special and I mattered.

It is interesting how people from different walks of life would relate to this story. It is a story that we have been told when we were young and it is still told today. It is about a fig tree which had no fruits. The fact that it had no fruits is immaterial, but it is about the power behind the words that even amazes anyone who hears about it. The strength of the word did not only dry up the leaves but it transcended all the way to its roots.

Nothing went to waste. Everything I received was put to good use; the good, the bad, and the ugly. It was not smooth sailing. Smooth sailing does not always happen. I would know. Ten years ago on a cruise, everything was wonderful. Unexpectedly, in the middle of the ocean, as if it was the Titanic again, a bad storm! All I said was Lord let this sea be calm, and surely it became calm. Seven days later we were in Miami. I am thankful to my creator for giving me the wisdom to understand what was going on. Some people adopt the labels they are given and give all their power away. There is immeasurable beauty in taking back your power, owning it, and choosing how your story should read. Remember, everyone sees things from their own perspective, so their view of you or opinion of you should not be seen as the truth.

I am urging you to pick up your compass, find your passion, and head towards your purpose. Be yourself. God planted something in everyone. You just have to find what was planted in you.

CANADA

Monica Kunzekweguta is a multiple Best-Selling Co-Author. She is an International Speaker, Certified Life Coach, and Mastermind facilitator. She is the owner and founder of ACT TO GROW, a life coaching business. Additionally, she built a company called A Woman's Beauty: the name was inspired by the message in her book. Monica is Project Founder of Inspiration for Kids International, a charity which provides library books to children living in rural Zimbabwe. A Sociology graduate, who moved to the United Kingdom in 1994, Monica has worked there as a manager in the Mental Health sector for many years. Her resume includes several self-development and leadership courses, and uses her experiences in life to help others reach their potential.

https://www.facebook.com/monica.kunzekweguta
Email: monicasbookproject@gmail.com

CHAPTER 2 Tracy Kadungure

Appreciating My Homeland Heritage

Beauty is in the depth of a woman's soul and in the understanding of her roots and that spark one can't put her finger on.

I was born in Africa, the continent was also born in me, and so the love affair with my homeland began. Zimbabwe is home to Victoria Falls, one of the seven wonders of the world and the mighty Zambezi, which meanders its way across southern Africa and the Great Zimbabwe ruins; a unique authentication to the Bantu civilization of the Shona people. Legend concludes that it was the capital city of Queen of Sheba and a renowned trading centre.

Zimbabwe has a rich artistic tradition of learning through songs, dance, poems, stories, proverbs, literature, and arts and crafts. Each ethnic group has its own myths, legends, and heroes such as Lobengula, Kaguvi, and Mbuya Nhehanda, a spirit medium of the Zezuru people. They are national symbols and are a record of the clan's origins, traditions, and history.

My name is "Zivai". It is cute, and comes with a deep meaning: *"You Should Know"*. It raises my self-esteem and a sense of belonging to my clan. I am forever Africa. The blood of Africa runs through my veins and the beat of drums resonates in my bones, in my blood, echoing in the rhythm of my beating heart. I have a deep, reverential sense of respect for marvels that surrounds me. I am in awe of the wonders of the sun, the moon, and stars.

I am a Nubian Goddess, Queen, Mother Earth, and every woman. My Africanesque body shape has curves in all the right places. My skin is color of dark chocolate. My soft curly hair is my crowning glory. I owe my being to the hills, valleys, mountains, rivers, deserts, fauna and flora, and the ever-changing seasons that define the face of my native land. My childhood is rooted in oral culture. The tradition of storytelling makes it possible for a culture to pass knowledge, history, and experiences from one generation to the next.

I am a child, girl, daughter, sister, friend, lover, wife, mother, and much more. I am the giver of life and unconditional love; a saver and source of nurturing, devotion, and patience. Putting my people before me is the essence of a supernatural being. Goddess inside me understands that death should not be feared, but is part of life, birth, and renewal.

In Africa, most tribes have animals they regard as their totems. I am my name, my surname, and above all I am my Totem. *Shava/Mhofu yemukono, Nhuka, Mhukahuru* is Shona name for the noble Eland. The majestic Eland is my totemic animal spirit guide. It walks the earth with you in spirit form and serves as a representation for family, clan, lineage, and tribe. It walks the sacred path, honoring every aspect of life. It provides strength, energy, and power to one who is called by its Totem. It commands respect and portrays wisdom of the mind. It brings the clan closer to the source of life; the cradle of their birth. It assists the clan to hold to their roots, principles of loyalty, family, and social obligation to heart. Family take precedence above all other matters in life. Commitments once made are kept with honor. It is a spirit of survival and feels the nominated with gratitude, consistency, strength, stability, blessing, prosperity, power, tranquility, and abundance.

I am African. My people hold me in their love and special places in their hearts. I stand with mother earth and honor her abundant provision. My totem is Shava. It is a variant of Mhofu/Mpofu which is the name of the animal Eland common in Southern Africa. It helps me establish a deep connection to the earth and will ask me to help the endangered species of our planet. I achieve nothing without the aid of the spiritual realm of the Eland. He brings me strength of and that gratitude is expressed to every part of creation.

Mine was a happy childhood filled with love, laughter, and a care free way of life with all the children belonging to the community. The parents had a responsibility in the rearing of the children even if they did not conceive and bear them. They raised us with their own values, some of which we dismiss as old fashioned as we grew older. But they were able to do so in a society that provided safe places to play, food to eat, schools, and economic opportunities to support them. Collectively, the parents built that world for all the children in their community.

Each group of people have customs that are unique to them. However, in all ethnic groups throughout Africa, the family unit is of the utmost importance and it is reflected in the customs of each tribe. Family is the foundation of Zimbabwean society and gender roles are defined within the patriarchal male-headed household. Marriage is an important rite of passage, a sacred practice, and a symbol of graduation into adulthood. Death and burial mark a person's passage into the world of the living dead: that of the ancestors.

Rituals play an important role in African social and cultural life. Both boys and girls go through rites of passage, which mark their coming of age or achievement of adulthood. Rites and ceremonies also accompany courtship and marriage, seasonal events, and death. Rites of passage provide the African with the foundation of his or her being; identity, sexual identity, and the roles of gender identity are enriched through the rites of passage. The men are prepared for their responsibility in the community and the women are prepared for their responsibility in the nation. Older women were appointed to help young girls understand the process of menstruation and what it entails in terms of hygiene. Periods are a sign of maturity – that is when girls are equipped for adult life.

I was taught the basic skills of life and roles of a woman in society, such as respect for the husband and in-laws when I got married. I was also taught socio-cultural norms that include dating, sexual conduct, self-reliance, brewing beer, ritual ceremonial duties, and the use of African medicines. This was to realize my place in my society and as a woman I had to play a subordinate role. I was expected to serve my husband, bear him children, and be part of his clan. When I began dating, he introduced me to his family and I introduced him to my aunts and grandmother. They asked questions about his intentions.

Marriage is one of the core fundamentals of nation building. There is no civilization that has ever existed that abstained from nuptials. African weddings are traditional, spiritual, and social family affairs. It is the uniting of two lives, two families, and their communities. The marriage customs of the Shona people of Zimbabwe is a process of several months. In due course Roora, bride price was paid by my future husband. It is an amount of money, property, or other form of wealth paid by a groom to the parents of the woman he is marrying as a gesture of sincerity. This is similar to the modern engagement ring except that the *bride price* goes to the woman's family. Traditionally, lobola was paid in cattle, a valued commodity in many African cultures, but today many modern couples pay lobola in cash. Lobola is intended to bring together two families, fostering mutual respect. It also indicates that the groom is financially capable of supporting his wife. The negotiations of lobola can take a few hours with the persons sent as diplomatic representatives, vanyayi going back and forwards and passing on messages until a common ground was reached.

When the marriage ceremony was in motion, some appointed women were given the task of teaching me the art of splendor sex. My waist was adorned with colourful waist beads. These were meant to entice my husband into romantic sexual conduct and served as sexual stimulant. I was taught the bedroom dance because I was expected to be sexually active and participate in my husband's pleasure. I had to recite my man's totem, chidawo during love making to arouse pleasure and to thank him for the privilege of being his wife.

I also took certain medicines to strengthen virility. I was expected to have a basic knowledge of herbs to cure ailments such as headaches, stomach aches, menstrual pains, and the like. I had to make sure that my husband was satiated. Because of these sexual skills, sexual life must be sweet at all times without exception. In preparation for married life, I was given a bowl for water to wash myself and my husband after love making. I was also provided with a flannel and small calabash with scented oils called Chinu to rub over my husband's body.

My aunts, sisters, and I arrived the day before the ceremony just as the sun set. We stood outside the homestead. Traditionally, my face was covered with a white cloth. Then with every few steps I took my intended's family paid monies for me to enter into the homestead. My journey ended in my mother-in-law's thatched round kitchen. Once inside the hut more monies were paid for me to remove the cloth. When my people were satisfied with the monies presented, I was unveiled and people saw my face for the first time and I greeted my in-laws. That was when my man's family got to see my face for the first time. They began ululating and singing songs, telling how happy they were that I was joining their clan and was going to have babies for their son.

A big party of introductions, eating, dancing, and drinking went on into the morning. The feasting commenced with traditional brew, meat, and food. The dance movements were of a sexual nature; mimicking courtship and sexual encounters and exhibiting sexual prowess of both men and women. That night, I did not share the bedroom with my intended. Instead, I spent the night with my own relations who continued telling me the dos and don'ts of a married woman.

My entourage woke up early to sweep the homestead yard, and money was given to us in appreciation of the work. After sweeping, we gave all the member of the family water to bath while more money was given. When the guests were gathered, I was escorted by my sisters to be formally presented to the people. The introductions were followed by speeches by my people and my husband's people. The two families prepared and shared sadza, made with maize meal, black jack, rice with peanut butter, beef, chicken and sadza cooked with millet. The foods signified the acceptance of new relations between the two families. Friends and relatives took that opportunity to give us wedding presents. The groom's family sought permission from my aunt for my husband to take me as his wife. When permission was granted, the function came to an end.

With the sole purpose of helping the transition to married life and settlement in my new home, appointed relatives stayed with me for a few days.

UNITED KINGDOM

Tracy Kadungure was born in Bulawayo, Zimbabwe. She taught in elementary schools before migrating to England. From the day she arrived, Tracy juggled jobs, from cleaning and working in the shops to Care work. When she retired, she was a Resource Manager in a Day Centre for one of London's leading Councils. Tracy loves an eclectic mix of Romance, Mystery, Thriller, Fantasy, and Reality, to name a few. A passionate story teller, she is a published author of Tanaka Chronicles, a trilogy of Erotic stories about a girl's journey through the labyrinth of growing up and her voyage of sexual discovery from girl to womanhood.

https://www.facebook.com/TracyKadungureNovelist/?fref=ts
Email: tkadunguparker@yahoo.co.uk

CHAPTER 3 Zothile Tatenda

The Bond between Mother and Child

Everyone has a past — a series of events or maybe just one event that could have changed you. Many of us go through rough patches and we come out stronger on the other side. But some of us are not so lucky. We come out crippled, bashed, and bruised. Some of you are still in your storm and are losing hope, but speaking from a family that came out crippled, bashed, bruised, AND stronger than ever, I encourage you to hold on.

I remember the day I saw my mum cry. Not just tears but it was like her heart was bleeding out through her eyes. I saw agony and heartbreak through each tear and I honestly didn't know what to do. I sat there. Quiet. Stunned. And in total fear. You see, my mum was the type of woman to only cry when something has shredded her heart. She was a strong and determined woman and in my opinion, probably had an IQ of a million. Seeing her so broken made me wonder what exactly had ripped out the spark out of her.

They say that when someone messes with your mind, they are messing with your greatest and most valuable asset. When someone can shake you to the core, where you get mentally injured, then they have crippled you. That's exactly what happened. She took a beating to the mind. A king hit to her self confidence. An elbow strike to the memory. But worst of all, she was dragged through a pit of emotional despair that no human should ever go though. That's exactly what workplace bullying does. It takes away a piece of someone that can never be replaced. It ruins a family. It makes a small girl aged thirteen turn into the substitute mum of the house.

What do you think of when you remember your childhood? Hugs and kisses? The smell of happiness when mum and dad are cooking? Fun in the sun and ice-cream till your heart's content? Being a child is an exhilarating experience. I always thought that childhood was the best part of a person's life. Being the oldest, I sort of envied my little brothers and sisters because they still got to run around and its hakuna matata all year round.

I had that feeling of euphoria and static glow of youth until it came to an abrupt halt, someone hit the brakes and then hit accelerate and I went from being thirteen-years-old to seventeen in a month. You probably think that I'm being over dramatic. You're probably rolling your eyes right now, thinking about how crazy this sounds. But it's all true. You see, I had to grow up fast so that I could become the crutch for my mum. I had to learn four years' worth of lessons in four months. I had to leave my small size six shoes and step into large clown shoes that I was meant to wear four years later.

Maybe this will all make more sense if I back track.

Okay, let's start in the year 2005. Mum and Dad had just told us that we are going to move to Australia…PERMANANTLY! We had been back and forth between Australia and Africa for my whole life. I loved Australia so to me it was like a giant lollypop had just fallen out of the sky and onto my dinner plate. I was born in Zimbabwe, Africa, a place where gorgeous outfits and amazing hairstyles are bound to drop jaws. Sunday was my favorite day and everyone dressed in the most immaculate way possible. We weren't afraid to dress our best; it was the day we went to the house of The Lord. When we were in Australia, we were based in Perth. Perth was a hot place and we frequently visited the beach. The beach holds a lot of happiness and joy for me. I was only little but memories of the beach family time will stick with me forever. Growing up in two different cultures, learning two different languages was engaging and exciting. I was simply never bored.

Anyway, so the day came when we were about to set off to build a home in Australia. You know the saying "African time", yeah um, we nearly missed the plane. None the less we landed safely and by the grace of God the plane did not catch on fire. The first thing we ate in Australia was a McDonald's meal. Don't judge us. It was conveniently waiting for us in the Airport. You know how it is. So we settled in well and life went as planned for a few years. I got a boyfriend…mum said no and that was the end of that chapter. Very quick stage of my life. The point is, we were happy. I had room to make mistakes and fix them. Nothing about my early years was out of the ordinary. We were content.

Mum was an amazing business orientated woman and Dad was a man of technology; both of them are super smart. So genetically, I have to be super smart too. You know how Africans are. The only jobs accepted are Doctor, Lawyer, Dentist, Information Technology Business Analyst, etc. I, on the other hand, wanted to be an actress. I had been in school plays and loved the stage so much that I wanted it as my job. But from day one, they had plans. I was already going to be a woman of a thousand talents in their eyes. Why have one profession when you can have many. My parents were both driven and extremely talented people. Both capable of looking after the amazing family we had.

So a few years later, mum got a job as a Branch Manager and she couldn't be more excited. It was an opportunity for her to share her expertise and skills with other people so they could better themselves as well. She saw it as a huge door for even greater success. But not everyone saw her as an opportunity to learn and excel but rather a threat to their own position in the company. This is where the downhill started for us as a family. You see, this person did not only feel threatened and insecure in their job but they decided to take action and simply get rid of her all together. It seemed that they vowed to make life a living hell for her. This started a series of events that led straight to a pit of unhappiness that we would be stuck in for years. First, they started stealing credit for work that my mum had worked long days and nights to achieve, then came the constant criticism, isolation, and segregation. She then ganged up with others and they pounced on my mom like a pack of wolves. These events would ring in my mother's mind for years to come. This was the most painful part. One of our basic human needs is to be loved and wanted, and as much as people want to deny it, it affects people psychologically. Look at the great lengths that people go to, simply so that they can find a friend. And then when people lose one friend, they think about them for years. Some people spend half their lives looking for that one friend that they cherished. Imagine having no one. No friend. No one to talk to in a place full of people. No one smile at you when you walked in. People would stay away from her simply so that they didn't lose their jobs. Racist remarks were thrown at her and they took a stab at our family. This person tormented and constantly attacked my mum and the end result: post-traumatic stress disorder, tinnitus, anxiety, depression, loss of confidence and a lawsuit. I had lost the main woman in my life, emotionally. Instead of her being my rock, I had to step up and become her rock.

Things weren't the same anymore. Mum kept to herself. Locked away in her room. She was no longer the vibrant, outgoing person that she was. Dad took on a heavier load and was becoming strained. He worked so hard to support the family and constantly worrying about bills. The lawsuit started to drain the life out of our family. We were living day by day, wishing that things could go back to the way they were. For a long period of time we settled into a routine of lawyers meetings, doctors' appointments, prescriptions, pills and feeling anger, pain, and resentment. We were in our darkest time: being emotionally exhausted. Using credit cards to buy bread. So far behind on payments, we could only afford to pay $15 on a bill one month. We were drained. Hurt and feeling alone. As I said before, I am the oldest of the children. So it was my responsibility to keep it together. I knew we were struggling but I could not afford to let the little ones worry. My parents and I couldn't let them see the deep hole we were being dragged into. But I had to carry the burden. I didn't complain. I just needed to be strong and my mum to know that I could cope. But deep down, I was scared out of my mind. I mean, I was a kid for crying out loud. A kid that needed to assume the role of second in charge because of some heartless person who probably has no idea what sorrow they had brought upon our family.

You know, there was a point when I thought that, I was the problem. And that my mum kept to herself because of me. You know how children get in situations such as this. They begin to blame themselves. They justify their reason for blaming themselves. That's what I did. I always thought that, if I had told my mum to leave the job earlier then this bully would not have been able to hurt us the way they did. Maybe I should have made up a fake illness so mum wouldn't go into the branch on the days that she was most hurt. I thought about how I could have stopped her from going to work all together for a few months if I had just broken my arm or leg, or something. I should have done something.

Over the past five years, I have come to realize that this wasn't in my hands. It wasn't my fault. I couldn't have done anything to stop it. It says in the Holy book that everything happens for a reason. Our lives are not a coincidence or an accident. We were meant to be here. All I know is that, if I wasn't here, mum wouldn't be here. The thoughts of suicide would have kept on developing, manifesting, and eating her up if I didn't cut the roots. I was always reminding her that we serve a higher power and that all we can do is have faith in The Lord our God.

There is a love between mother and daughter that no one else can comprehend. Certain bonds that not even a husband can have. They are tailored for situations such as this. I would do anything for my mum. And I know, hands down, that my mum would do anything for me. There are no mountains too great for me to climb for her. No storms that I would not go through with her. I would never wish upon anyone else what happened to her. I wouldn't wish it upon the people who did this to her. No human being should ever have to go through what we went through.

One of my main encouragements is that we are never put through trials and challenges that we are unable to handle. It is much easier to say that now than a few years ago. Now I can honestly say that we have never been as strong as we are now. Yes, we bear the scars of a battle. We have come out with missing limbs and crippled, but nothing on earth is stronger than the heart of a fighter. There are many times when we could have given up and countless times when we could have just walked away, but my mum always told me to fight. So I am going to continue to fight for her until the war has been won.

AUSTRALIA

At eighteen, Zothile Tatenda is already an author, University Medical Sciences student and a qualified Financial Planner. She aspires to be a Life Coach. Her leadership skills can be tracked back to early years as a School Prefect. This led to being a Peer Support Leader by year nine. She was also involved in School Drama Productions, one of her most valued passions. At College, Zothile co-founded support networks for girls. She believes that God never gives us trials that we cannot handle. As a result, she has developed a tough character in her due to wisdom beyond her age.

zothile_tatenda@yahoo.com.au
zoe.smileyy@gmail.com

CHAPTER 4   Joy Mutare

Courage to Heal – Lessons from My Mother

The opportunity to contribute my story to this phenomenal project gave me cause to hesitate for various reasons, among them being reminders of my past failures, feelings of inferiority, sheer self-doubt and numerous other defeatist thoughts emanating primarily from my lived realities and reinforced by some who are closest to me whose opinions I have placed considerable value on. These severe judgments have not only been paralyzing, they have elevated themselves enough to drown any redeeming ones I have tried to entertain. They have led me to violently eject whichever thought dared me to consider the possibility of my personal story being of any interest, significance, or encouragement to anyone. Not only that but attempts to entertain the idea of there being a reminiscent glimmer of some light that may be present in my soul dissipate as fast as they arise, rendering this project immensely challenging.

The longer I have allowed my shortcomings to fester and marinate, the more I have begun to recognize the all too familiar trends I have permitted to become part of my life, a) holding myself to standard set by others, b) comparing myself to my contemporaries, c) succumbing to fear, and d) second guessing myself on every major life decision.

I have become convinced that only the spiritually mature, only they who have overcome various forms of hardship, who have learnt to forgive, have found serenity and continue to thrive; only they who enjoy economic prowess such as the likes of well-known public figures and so forth, they who have struggled through and overcome life's challenging odds presented by such situations as difficult childhoods can provide worthy, inspirational narrative.

Though I have allowed myself to wallow in self-pity, allowed fear to paralyze me, I have simultaneously founded a courage; have given myself permission to tell part of my own story with the disclaimer that *A luta continua*. So, I write; for the likes of me I write, for they who believe that one has to have overcome insurmountable odds to contribute to the literary world, I write, for the likes of me with little to no confidence and have low to no self-esteem at all I write – those who judge themselves too harshly and need reminders of how much the God who made us in their image loves us so, so much, I write! For the likes of me who are in pain, who consider themselves as failures and question their relationship with this God, I write.

Also, I write for all my encouragers; my direct and indirect, my conscious and unconscious, subtle and overtly enthusiastic cheerleaders whose dedication and faithfulness to me has repeatedly confirmed that angels do come in human form. However, since we kind of expect angels to be perfect anyway, I therefore acknowledge and stand in awe of those humans who purposefully serve others. I stand in awe of the humans God placed in my life who love me deliberately, defend my well-being with a tenacity untold and believe in me. I write for those who have sacrificed much in order to support my family and I. Receiving such a high caliber of devotion and commitment from a team so passionately cheering for me has helped me find meaning in what others call clichés. Because of my team's devotion to my wellbeing, I march on.

One of these Aces in my hand of life comes in the form of my sister Monica Kunzekweguta. As we discussed my participation in this project, I expressed how my recent and past failures disqualify me from being a worthy contributor to this project to which she responded, "Joy, I am convinced that you would not be calling yourself a failure unless someone else has said this to you first."

From this conversation, I concluded healing takes courage. I decided I want to heal because the pain hurt too much. I decide now to believe those who claim writing is therapeutic - but where to begin?

Gladys – The Early Years

After a grueling four days of labor, with the assistance of a skeletal but experienced staff of nurses in a small and ill equipped clinic in Victoria Falls, Zimbabwe, Constance Mutare gave birth to a bouncing baby girl to be known as Gladys Nontombi Mutare on July 22nd, 1971. From photographs, I can deduce that my parents had a nice wedding though I possess no vivid memories of ever living in the same house as my biological father. Therefore, my earliest childhood memories start in Chief Mutambara's village of Nhedziwa with my maternal grandparents Zienzile and Bekapi Albert Sithole around 1975/1976.

Though I was shielded from most of it, I could tell my mother's life was in marital and career turmoil. My grandparents' home was thus the sanctuary of stability I needed while my mother resettled from Victoria Falls where she and my father had lived, to the township of Mabvuku, Harare where she would acquire a teaching job at Mabvuku Primary School in 1977.

The raging Zimbabwean war of liberation increased my grandparents' anxiety for my safety. At their request to my mother, I relocated to Mabvuku in 1978 to not only escape this war but also to begin Grade One. Despite my family's "mother hen" protectiveness, I distinctly remember my mom's name change from Mutare to Sithole blatantly signaling to me that the marriage I never knew had ended – coming to think of it, as I now write these line, I can't hold back tears as I reflect on the fact that at this point in my life until I was much older I did not have a memory of my father's face and could not pick him out in a crowd where I asked to.

Despite my current sadness, back then, no significant emotions came over me one way or the other regarding my mother's divorce but at that young age, I had the sociological sensitivity to realize that stigma would attach to my mother as a divorcee since patriarchal societies such as Zimbabwe do tend to attach a woman's worth to her marital status.

In 1979, my mother caught the eye of a debonair court interpreter. I remembered him remarking to my mother's sisters, "I couldn't believe that this man was 'throwing away' such a gem of a woman." They would marry in 1980; my mother and I would move to the township of Highfield to live with my new dad and sadly, in 1981 after six months of a blissful marriage, he would be murdered and my mother and I would move to Glen View where they had purchased a home.

How dare I describe my mom's six month marriage as blissful? My dad **WAS** a doting husband! Because my mother still worked in Mabvuku, a two fare commute from Highfield, he and I would stroll to the bus stop to meet her and walk back home for a dinner he had already prepared. His affection for my mother was unquestionable, he shopped for her and to the day mom's body died thirty-three years later, I had kept some of the clothes he bought because their quality was that good and they lasted that long.

Further, I do not know if this was because his older biological children had started their own families that in nine year old me he embraced a second chance to father because he was phenomenal. My green school uniform was always meticulous, iron pressed to perfection; my dad polished and laid out my shoes and white socks every evening for me to wear the next day. Not only this, he dusted his old bookcase polished that too and made it school ready for me. I was always so immaculate that in keeping with Zimbabwe's 80's tradition – that whenever the President of Zimbabwe returned from one of his foreign missions or a dignitary visited the country, schools selected children to go to the airport to greet them; I was chosen to be among the children going to the airport for this occasion. I wonder if that still happens.

Anyway, it goes without saying that six months we had with my dad were priceless. It taught me what the face of unconditional love might look like. This year, also made tougher by the passing of my gorgeous eleven-month-old cousin, Comfort, found us in Glen View also afforded me an early introduction to patriarchy and a face-to-face encounter with the brokenness of mankind. It seemed not to matter that Constance held a legitimate marriage license and was the rightful owner of her house, as a woman who had not borne children by this marriage my dad's family promptly disqualified my mother from occupying the house and sought to evict her despite her mournful state.

Constance waged a brave inheritance battle and thankfully being educated and having the law on her side left this family with not a greedy leg to stand on. Legal merit didn't deter my dad's family from taking possession of all the furniture though; all but the bed she and my dad slept on and the TV my mother had bought after my dad's death. For Constance, it mattered little that we ate our meals sitting on the floor, as long as we were together and had a roof over our heads.

Gladys - Fast Forward 2014

My maternal grandmother would rename me Joylyn in 1983. I considered the dropping of my middle name, Nontombi as the only downside from this name change. In the coming years, I would graduate from the University of Zimbabwe in 1995; immigrate to the US in 1997 kind courtesy of Pierre Sutton, his amazing family and Inner City Broadcasting Corp. I would have my first born son, Munyaradzi in 2001, enroll in the MBA program at Syracuse University in 2004, the Sociology PhD program that same year, marry Samuel in 2006 and have my second and third children; Thabela in 2007 and Yinka in 2009 respectively. I founded ProjectItTakesaVillage, Inc. in 2004, all the while teaching at Lemoyne College, Syracuse University, Onondaga Community College and Cazenovia College where I currently find myself.

While these activities indicate God's immense blessings and unmerited favor, I forgot my one of my mother's best biggest teachings – humility. I tell the story of my upbringing yes, primarily to brag on my fantastic family. I tell it also to parallel the sheltering and super protection I received to that of Joseph, favorite son of Jacob as told in the book of Genesis. I tell it as backdrop to highlight that, like Joseph, not only did I forget to remain humble, my immaturity and conceitedness found me utterly unprepared to manage and crises brewed quickly.

This summer, another superb woman and good friend released her own book, she and I conversed at length regarding this project. I informed her that because that I am still going through my "situations" and am still trying to make my way to the other side makes me strongly believed I am not the best candidate to tell inspirational stories.

For today, I decide to gather the ammunition provided by my mother, my family as well as my cheerleaders in order to stop the hemorrhaging brought on by poor decision making, sheer stressors of life, self-doubt, pride, rebellion, and unwillingness to let God be a priority. I chose to give marriage, parenting, teaching, schooling and living another shot. I thank God for second chances, and sometimes third because only He can. I am ready to heal; ready to rediscover my identity, reclaim what I have lost. I am ready to repair the damage I have caused where I can with the tools I have been given. The outcome is still unfolding but for now, I will dedicate this project to Constance Sithole (1946-2013) who humbly loved and served others purposefully and deliberately. Her life inspires me and all who were close enough to her to catch some of her light as she passed through life.

UNITED STATES

Joy Mutare was born, raised, and educated in Zimbabwe, and migrated to the United States in 1997. While working at Inner City Broadcasting Corporation, Joy served at the largest HIV/AIDS support agency in New York. As she was studying for an M.B.A. at Syracuse University in 2002, Joy decided to become more academically and socially engaged in civil society. She founded an organization that supports the needs of children impacted by HIV/AIDS at her former school, as well as the school formerly taught by her mother. Joy Mutare teaches Sociology at Cazenovia College and Onondaga Community College, and lives in Cazenovia with her family.

http://www.pitav.org.
E-mail: tobeablessing@pitav.org

CHAPTER 5   Ruvarashe Ruzive

Abused, but Not a Victim

Through the different experiences life has thrown at me, I have come to believe that no one came to this earth to live, pay bills, and die. I believe that God did not waste HIS time intricately designing each human, selecting even the right pitch of voice and the wonderful details that make each person unique, so that you and me may come down to this wonderful planet just to add to the population. Even you my darling, in all your self-adoration, cannot supply me with the number of hairs on your head. But HE knows in the words of Matthew 10:30, *"But the very hairs of your head are all numbered."* Surely you cannot look me in the eye and tell me that HE went to all those lengths to create meaningless purposeless beings. I strongly believe that there is a reason for your existence and THAT my friend, THAT reason is your purpose.

Therefore, after the Lord went to such great lengths to create you and give you a purpose to fulfill, there is no way he was going to let you be raised by mediocre parents. Our parents were handpicked by God as the perfect catalysts for the materialization of our destinies. When God created us, he even elected our parents as the best mentors to instill and develop the necessary values and qualities in us to make us who we are destined to become. Dear friend, let me tell you today that you were born in the right era. You were born right on time to fulfill the purpose that God created you to fulfill. Take my hand and I follow as I take you on a journey. This is my story…

On the fourth of October, 1995, my mother shuffled her way to the Mine Hospital. She was worried. Her long awaited child whom she and my father had struggled seven good years to finally have had been lying motionless in her belly for a few days. She had been hoping that after her first Caesarian Section, her second child would be born naturally. However, as she sat facing the doctor on that fateful day that dream was fast slipping out of her grip. The doctor raised his eyes from his clipboard, faced her solemnly, and broke it to her in a monotone that she was going to be having an emergency C-section. In that single moment two dreams were shattered into a million tiny pieces like broken glass. Her dream of giving birth naturally was destroyed as was the prospect of having any more children as it is medically stated that a woman is only allowed two Caesarian Sections in her life. Anything beyond two is considered high-risk and life-threatening. I was born on that very day.

My parents have done a wonderful job as mentors. In me, they have raised a strong-willed and independent young lady who is reaching for he stars. Destined for Greatness. From a young age, I was taught that nothing is impossible. I was groomed to believe that if I wanted something and if I thought I could attain it, I should disregard society's rules and get it. To critically analyze and question everything and not just take what I was told is another great attribute they instilled in me. My mother is my safe place and my father is my Greatest Icon. My name Ruvarashe translated to English, means "The King's Flower" and indeed I grew up a protected and treasured life, truly fit for any King's favorite flower. My parents sent me to Pre-school early and I did well there competing with my peers. After just two years of pre-school, my father was satisfied with my tenure and decided that I was ready for "Big School". Even my Pre-School teachers agreed that I was too bright to spend another year with them. Therefore, I graduated from Pre-School that December with people a class ahead of me.

The following year, I started Big School donned in my little blue tunic. I felt "big" and clever, even though I was five years old and all my peers were a year older. The most exciting time for me each year was my birthday in October when I would turn a year older and catch up with them for a few months before they got older than me again. In October 2002, I was in Grade two already and I had just caught up with my peers. I was feeling very grown up and basking in my temporary equality with my school peers. It was about a week after my birthday and I was still half expecting some more birthday presents from my remaining family and friends. Anyhow, I was walking around the vast expanse of my father's walled territory, safely nestled inside his gates from the world's terrors that were locked outside. I had been told that I shouldn't leave the yard because it was unsafe outside. Indeed I felt safe because my father was the strongest man and he could beat any monster. I trusted him when he said I was safe in there so I walked freely without any worry. Nothing could catch me there! Boy was I wrong!

Three male members of my family were hanging out by one of my fathers' buses. They were the new Dandy watermelon flavored bubblegum. As a child I was obviously interested besides, we shared a surname with these young men and I was still expecting a birthday present from them. Three measly pieces of gum that I couldn't even bring myself to eat afterwards – that is what I traded my innocence and childhood for. They hoisted me up suddenly from the ground but I wasn't alarmed as I thought it was the "yavenyamayekugocha" game where one adult grabs my arms and the other takes my feet then they swing me from side to side singing the song. Evidently that wasn't the plan as the other guy placed his hand forcefully on my mouth. Two of them exchanged turns with me, hurting me in ways I didn't understand. All I could do was cry, but there was a hand firmly clamped on my mouth, therefore I could not make any noise. The last one could not get himself to violate me. He was the one who had his hand clamped on my mouth. I guess after he had felt my tears, he couldn't get himself to do it. It happened two more times before my mother noticed a withdrawal in my character as well as a change in my gait. A sort of limp.

After what those three men had done to me, I was alone in the world and I could not trust anyone. I realized during that horrid experience that I was not safe anywhere in the world – not even in my father's territory. It was all a farce. A fantasy. It took a lashing with my mother's belt to get me to finally break it to her in tears. She was gutted. The child she had waited seven good years to finally hold had been robbed of the one thing money could not buy. My innocence and my childhood. My father wept. I saw my father cry! The invincible man, even he was destroyed by the news. Doctor's reports confirmed three counts of rape. I admire my father for the decision he took on the issue. He decided it was best for the family if the case did not go to court. At the time he was a public figure and this kind of publicity was bad for his public role. It was also difficult for him to send members of his own family to jail. That choice had the capacity to ruin family bonds. It was a wise decision but I didn't know it at the time.

I understand it now because of 1st Corinthians 10:13, which says, *"No temptation has seized you that is not common to man. And God is faithful; HE will not let you be tempted beyond what you can bear."* My parents raised me in a way that empowered me. Although I thought I couldn't handle it at the time, God was sure of me. He elected these two parents as the right parents for me and every choice they made that time made me who I am today. If God trusted them, who was I to disagree.

The fact that they didn't treat me as my past was the best gift they could have given me. They raised me to believe that being abused is not disability and even disability in itself is not inability. To be a victim of abuse is to let it define you and even deprive you of other things because you believe it is a limiting factor. My parents raised me to be a Victor of child abuse because they treated the abuse as something ordinary. Sometimes we amplify our problems and by doing that, we let them get bigger than us even to the point of destroying or crippling us. To prove just how much they empowered me, I was even elected prefect in Grade 6 at my primary school. I became a leader and even attained 5 points in my Grade 7 examinations because they empowered me. I never went through life feeling sorry for myself and sometimes I feel that that is the worst thing we can do for our children and ourselves. We should never brand ourselves weak and crippled by our circumstances. In the process, we destroy any fight left in ourselves.

From looking back to the child my parents were raising me to be in my pre-school years, I learnt that age, race, and all these other categories the society has constructed do not limit the capacity of your greatness. I have always been with people way out of my league in terms of society's categories but I have gone in and thrived. In High School, my parents awarded me the opportunity of being in a private school. That experience resulted in me attaining wonderful A levels, I was elected prefect yet once again, I received half colors in Debating, a certificate in Toastmasters amongst many other decorations that fill a folder today. My parents enabled me to do all these things because of the way they raised me. This is why I trust God as being the one that selects the right mentors for us to be raised to fulfill our purpose. At the age of nineteen, I have already begun fulfilling my purpose. You dear friend are reading my written words as one of the important people I need to make my purpose a reality. I thank you.

After I completed my high school in 2013, I took a gap year in 2014 to gain work experience and wouldn't trade my experience for anything in the world. It has matured me and changed my perspective on life completely, changing my mindset. My direct overhead is a young recently wed man with one son. He is only left with about twenty years before retirement. He has only worked less than ten years and a general house loan requires up to twenty years of paying back. If he is going to get a loan, he will spend the rest of his working years paying for that house. I am nineteen and retirement age is fifty-five. I am left with only thirty-six years before retirement and I am not even ready for formal employment. I am Ruvarashe Ruzive. I WILL be great and you are invited to come with me on that journey.

Dear friend;

I want you to know that you are here for a reason. You have unlimited potential. God does not collect each tear that falls from your precious eyes (Psalms 56:5) so that you come to this world, finish your tenure, and fade with no sign of your existence. Close your eyes for a minute. If people had to write a statement summarizing your life, what would you want them to write? What have you done to make sure that those words become a reality? If nothing is done yet, THAT is your homework. Start today. You have greatness within you! Unleash it.

UNITED KINGDOM

Ruvarashe Ruzive is a remarkable twenty-year-old author who is currently pursuing an undergraduate course in England. This program will lead to a joint LLB in Law and Economics degree by December 2017. Since junior school, Ruvarashe has held numerous leadership positions. She is a Certified Toastmaster and has competed in many debate competitions. She holds certificates in International Relations, and also in Grooming and Etiquette. Ruvarashe posts regularly on her Facebook page, Untamed Greatness, where she shares a lot of wisdom based on her Christian values. She is passionate about people, and aims to help people understand their unlimited potential.

ruvaruzive@gmail.com
https://www.facebook.com/Ruvarashehonormarieruzive

CHAPTER 6   Melody Mbondiah

My Strength Comes From Within

This is a story of renewed strength after hitting rock bottom; how I bounced back despite a rocky marriage, delayed career progress, and a relationship with my faith. It will illustrate details of how I felt when I had lost my hair, but also how it grew back just like Samson in the Bible. Hair signifies your dignity. It is meant to protect you from the elements and a harsh environment. That is why you need it: on your head, on your skin, on your eyelids and all the sensitive areas of your body including inside your nose. In some cultures and religions, hair symbolizes the inner beauty of an individual and needs to be secured. Ask yourself some of the facts about hair and its use. You will find they are connected to covering, protecting etc. That is why I have written this chapter. My hair has been cut several times, but it also has grown beautifully. Life is indeed a journey but what has been significant to me is that I have not walked alone. I have traveled far and wide only to come back and learn that self-discovery is an immense tool in any individual's life, especially when questioning your true purpose.

I have often wondered what the benefit of a righteous life is; when life presents setbacks that challenge your faith to the point you see no physical breakthrough. I want to thank all pastors and Christians who have been a source of support and comfort in my times of struggle and indeed confusion as to my purpose in the Christian walk. I recognize that when one is called, the struggles are not little but huge. A wise man said when your purpose is large, the darts thrown at you seem like giants. He goes further to say that darts thrown at you only serve as opportunities for growth. If you stand on the word of God and confess who you really are in Christ, no devil in hell can stop your destiny.

I have written this story to encourage people from all walks of life to seek their purpose, to remember that everyone matters to God. Yes EVERYONE! If you ever mistreated someone or belittled them due to the struggles or difficulties they experienced, be assured that God has an appointed time for everyone and His will is that all people come to salvation to the Glory of His Name. One important fact of life is that everyone has a purpose and no one should stop it from fulfilment except God; hence humans must serve God by serving others. I encourage you to see your breakthrough which is imminent, because that purpose must be established as long as you search deep within yourself.

I want to encourage you that if you are in a seemingly dire situation and you find yourself cornered, rest assured that everything must happen to give Glory to God; even seemingly painful and disastrous times. A story is told of a man who had a terrible condition and people came to ask the Lord whose fault it was that the man was in that state. Jesus answered and said, "Neither this man nor his parents have faulted, but that the glory of God must be made manifest." This scripture encouraged me to know that unfortunate events had nothing to do with me, particularly where I knew for sure that I was clean of all the devil's accusations. This story will enable especially those who have strived to keep their walk righteous but experience affliction, for the bible says: *Many are the afflictions of the righteous but the Lord delivereth them out of them all.*

The Story

What was I thinking? Things never work out for me anywhere...if only my mother was alive I would have someone to confide in and draw strength from. But this, as cliché as it sounds, was the "story of my life". I had tried so hard in my adult life to make life better than it was growing up. My dad was a doting father who I love to pieces and my stepmother too – a patient woman. I had made a vow to myself...when I finished my A' levels, I would travel to a faraway country for University and live the life I always wanted by getting married to the most kind, God-fearing man the earth could give. Yet here I was in the UK, working towards my 2nd degree and growing strong in the Lord, but hey, that story of my life episode again.

When I met my ex-husband, I really didn't think marriage was on the cards any sooner. He proposed after three months of dating and I was excited and happily agreed. What I didn't know was that I would encounter several challenges in my marriage. Firstly, living in England meant my father could not be available to accept and be fully engaged in the traditional marriage ceremony "bride price" – hence he delegated some extended family members. That was just the tip of the iceberg as what followed was simply doom. I proceeded to marry what I perceived was the man of my dreams. But alas, God was not in it. To start with, the man's immigration status was not confirmed, hence I suffered for this as he often insulted me, blaming me for "slowing his papers". This man was impatient and soon his true colors began to show. After the birth of our son, things quickly went bizak with infidelity, emotional, and financial abuse. I was so distraught I felt empty inside. The number of times I just wanted to die grew countless. My ex-husband got so frustrated, he blamed my family and myself for the chaos. Through it all, we had domestic disputes that were irreconcilable. This is when my career was attacked, being a Social Worker prospect. I could not explain what was going on, let alone the loud cry of agony in my heart! Indeed something in me said, "One day you'll write about this and someone will be healed." So here it is – that promise of hope being fulfilled.

Working in social services, I witnessed statutory involvements daily on service users' lives and found it traumatic supporting families in distress while mine was crumbling. I had seen this too many times in my work for that awful dreaded moment when due to domestic disputes, families lose children. My faith deteriorated. I took time off my course, and my marriage ended. Having been a zealous youth in the things of God, I felt cheated. Why was this happening to me? Where was God? How come my life turned to be so miserable? I was just tired of it all, miles apart...too distant to ever be connected. I confessed to myself that I had failed and this was the last straw. I never wanted to be divorced and have a divided home, but this seemed to be "the story of my life". I remembered those days I spent toiling in the house of God, keeping myself for my future husband. Why hadn't I gone clubbing and enjoyed myself? What justice was there for me? I remembered the story in the book of Psalms, "Why do the wicked prosper?" Evil is out there. It does not want to see the best of you as mentioned in Ephesians 6. Unfortunately, anyone or anything surrounding you can be used by the devil, including marriage, friends and family, colleagues, etc., to attack you. Where I was and where I wanted to be were miles apart and I got past the point of depression to just existing in a life of uncertainty. I cannot begin to explain how sad, depressed, demotivated, and angry I was. I broke down on my knees and prayed for sanity. What was this? Questions raced in my head and I had nothing left inside of me. I felt ripped apart and those around me mentioned how I was edgy and snapped at them. Rational things became irrational.

But thank God for Jesus. I purposefully decided to choose what I wanted in my life – the life I wanted, the future I was purposed, and within the twinkle of an eye, my spirit focused on positivity. In my mind, I flushed out and rejected all the negatives in my life. I decided if this was not my marriage, then it too must be flushed out of my life. I made a deal with God and in that moment of chaos, I cried, "Lord, if this is not my portion." It's amazing what followed in that moment of time. I witnessed my ex-husband declare and admit that his intentions were amiss. That night he left and never came back again.

My journey to self-discovery was equipped by love, pain, experience, and knowing who I am in God. The whole episode existed to strengthen my faith to equip me and above all, it was a journey…the one I walked, suffered, and conquered! The lesson was quite simple, but to actually grasp its sanity was more than I was ready to experience. But how can we find ourselves when WE DON'T EXPERIENCE? To experience hardship is to seek the face of God because he is the Creator. Tomorrow is created by lessons learnt in the past and discovered today. I have learnt that emotions can never be trusted. When we act based on feelings, the solutions are temporary and dissatisfactory. However, when we act on moral basis and stand for what is right, God takes His place in our situations. No one has the right to lay hands on your visions and disrupt them, whatever the reasons. The truth of the matter is you were designed for greatness and any challenge you encounter will serve to your elevation. You will always look back and see God carrying you despite those who plot against you. Those who plot against you will mince every word spoken against you.

I found strength to overcome. I had renewed faith, business ideas came flowing in, and joy in my son. I began from the beginning, who I was in Christ and the legacy I wanted to live behind. I began to refocus my life and grow through what God had said I am. It's amazing that through difficult challenges in life, individuals can find strength in whom it originally came from – the Creator of the universe. I did not do anything new but draw closer to myself and God because not the best friends, Pastors, family, or holidays could do it. The person I was inside was coming out again, healing, and that journey to self-discovery was slowly created. God was trying to work something in me but the enemy had put barriers to the way I thought my life had mapped up. Today I am a happy International best-selling book author, declaring that God's word says, "His promises are yes and Amen."

I truly hope that any person who has blows in life thrown at them, recognize these as stepping stones. Create your journey and don't be bitter – move forward. In my home language, there is a proverb which states that while growing up, every child falls somewhere, somehow. But if the child does not rise again after the fall, it becomes a concern for the parents. God has put so much in us to be victorious. That means there is something out there to battle with and be victorious over. Today, decide. Make up your mind, whatever the circumstance: background limitations, financial challenges, emotional bruising, or psychological mind-set. Let it all go and start your journey afresh. My journey has taught me that it is not the beginning of a matter that's important, but how it ends! Indeed no matter how many times my hair is cut, like Samson, my strength does not go but rather comes back more immensely and I shall continue to conquer in Jesus' mighty name.

UNITED KINGDOM

Melody Mbondiah is a certified Life Coach who resides in the UK. She has experience in the Financial Industry in South Africa as well as a BA in Social Work qualification in the UK with several years' experience in the social care sector. As well, she successfully completed a Bcom Business Management Degree (Hrs). She currently runs her Coaching business "Goshen Business Solutions" through eliminating limiting beliefs while also working with the youth in her local Birmingham community. Mel has featured in the American magazine "The Belief Magazine" (January issue) and has co-authored two books currently best-sellers on Amazon.

www.goshenbusinesssolutions.co.uk
Email: brownmel@webmail.co.za

CHAPTER 7 Andrée Nicole

A Season of Faith's Perfection

A Season of Faith's Perfection was birthed out of my personal experiences, and remains to be a gift to me, as I hope that it will be to you as well. My source of inspiration comes from having the opportunity to share my story. In doing so, it has allowed me to experience a wealth of emotion, from fear, to sadness, to frustration, to anger, to joy, and then...happiness! More importantly, the concept of change and the beginning of a new path presented themselves to me. A Season of Faith's Perfection shows how I gained a tremendous amount of insight and I believe that it would be most beneficial for others to learn that they are not alone, that there is a light at the end of the tunnel, and that women can experience wholeness in every facet of their lives again.

My chapter speaks to women of strength, women of courage, and women of integrity. But more importantly, it conveys to Phenomenal Women who have taken many single steps of fear and replaced them with steps of faith in order to complete their journey. This motivational, inspirational, self-help story will propel you to a place that will hopefully give you a fresh new pair of eyes to see, like they have never seen before.

It is very important that I am able to share my real life story with all of you, because my voice had become silenced, and therefore the dialogue that was so full of life had also become muted and was replaced by a dialogue of unfamiliarity riddled with daily tests, trials, and tribulations. This compelling story is a source of inspiration that boils and bubbles as you, the readers, learn how I become refreshed, renewed, and restored while having to deal with life's daily challenges by means of rich determination and drive.

The challenges that I speak of are in reference to the year 2010, when I fell victim to a serious motor vehicle accident.

My change brought on confusion and mirrored a state of being constantly overwhelmed with the daily liberties of life. FEAR had set in and altered my perception of the things that were once perceived as being simple. Now, they became rather mundane and complex and the self-imposed limitations of my mind held me down, shackled me in bondage, and kept me as a prisoner. In doing so, the words that I had become familiar with and now uttered from my mouth had become cautious, yet inspired to speak from a broken place that entertained the depths of my being and my inner soul. A tender spirit silenced by trauma caused my single steps of physical, emotional, and spiritual well-being to become tainted, shattered, tampered with, and even unrecognizable to ME.

The change that I speak of happened in an instant with a thunderous clamor that jolted me in such an unexpected manner. This journey left an imprint on my mind, body, and spirit, and now my vehicle became tangled with another body of steel. It took me a moment to digest the severity of what had just occurred. On that wretched day, both air bags became deployed and stung my entire face, vehemently snapping my fragile head back against the car's headrest. Vapors and strong odors began to seep into the interior of the vehicle as it now adorned the traffic light pole that was situated on the curb of the sidewalk. Clear fluids ran profusely from my nose, my entire body ached from shock, and now what used to be an empty street began to fill up rather quickly with witnesses to this tragic event. I struggled with the opening of the vehicle door. After being unsuccessful with the third attempt, I began to panic, and for a quick moment, the thought of death entered my mind. On the fourth try however, I was able to regain my composure and successfully exited. I stumbled over my own feet in total disbelief of what my eyes had witnessed and made my way toward the grassy area. I stood totally numb adjacent to where the accident took place and remain thankful to this day that my life had been spared.

The gentlemen that caused the accident, along with the other people present at the scene, gathered around me and poured onto the sidewalk. He asked me if I was okay and I whispered to him that I was scared. I believe that seeing the traffic light dangling above the hood of my vehicle and also learning that because of this impact, the traffic pole had caused the power outage in the surrounding area contributed to that feeling of despair.

That very morning, before I made my way to work, my mother- in-law prayed for my son as well as my protection; she did not know that I would be a victim of an automobile accident. I later learned that my father, while traveling home from work, had seen the very same ambulance pass by him on the street not too far from where I was located. He did not realize that it was en route to me. My cousins, also on their way home in the surrounding vicinity, spoke about me for ten minutes before I fell victim to this accident – one that would literally change me forever.

Following my life-altering collision, I attended weekly doctor's and specialist's appointments with physiotherapists, chiropractors, insurance companies and adjusters to receiving acupuncture and massages, seeking MRIs, X-Rays, CAT scans, to being drowned in countless documents and paperwork. In response to this loss of control, I created barriers and mountains that ultimately blocked my ability to love and to care for others, even myself. Anguish saturated my entire body without my permission, and I became emotionless and, therefore, delved deeper within myself until I became paralyzed with FEAR.

With time, love, patience, and faith in HIM, another direction had presented itself to me and allowed order to creep in. This was a season of faith's perfection, and as each day, month, then year introduced itself to me...each season I became refreshed, renewed, and restored. This is when my steps of fear became replaced with steps of faith.

Faith grows best in the winter of trial and sings and dances ever so beautifully with CHANGE.

Some may describe a change in season as a subdivision of the year or as a significant difference in the weather, while others choose to identify this noticeable modification with the ecology of a particular hemisphere and the amount of hours of daylight in a given day. All in all, these seasons are marked by changes; how the intensity of the sunlight—or lack thereof—would reach the Earth's surface. I too had experienced these shifts within the four seasons.

During the winter season, animals hibernate while the plants lie dormant. Similarly, I too distanced myself from the not-so-kind days that were often riddled with immeasurable challenges and therefore found refuge in the arms of nature. In the midst of these trials, I was able to succumb to an environment filled with constant motion, activity, noise, and even turmoil. It was during these times that I began to develop a deep appreciation for these seasons of faith's perfections.

The tree that stood outside my bedroom window became very symbolic to me in the sense that to the naked eye, one would sight our beauty. Just like the tree, others would see the trunk, bark, branches, and leaves, yet many would fail to realize that underneath the earth are the roots that give it life and sustenance. The roots of this majestic tree represent my challenges – the constant rushing of thoughts, fears, anxieties, and sleepless nights endured by physical and emotional pain.

Winter

In the midst of this chaos, winter had symbolized death and stagnation. Loved ones and friends chose to see what they could see, not realizing how misguided they had become about my changes, beauty, strength, and ability to cope. Yet despite the darkness that was faced during these winter months, this season taught me the importance of faith, hope, and oneness. Perhaps it was the purity and freshness of the first snowfall that did it for me because when it snowed, all my cares and worries also became covered.

Snowstorms represent the trials and tribulations of my journey and remind me of the steps that I had taken; but more importantly, these steps had produced footprints that reminded me that I was never really ever alone. They illustrated to me that my Creator has always been there with me, had never forsaken or left me, and would always remain by my side. And because of this, I am most grateful for this winter wonderland.

Winter, Spring

Spring represents rebirth, a blossoming into one's life or period of growth when things appear fresh, bright, and promising. For me, this season exemplified a time of new beginnings and balance, and I learned that in order to move forward, I could no longer focus on or be continuously preoccupied with taunting thoughts of the past.

Springtime cleaning was the most necessary procedure in order for complete healing to take place. Therefore, during this season, I focused on cleansing my inner self before any of the outer self could ever become an inward treasure.

Winter, Spring, Summer

Summertime, on the other hand, embodied a time full of joy and happiness and I was finally able to relax and have some fun. This season denoted a time for my thoughts to be free and harmonized with life itself once more.

Despite the sweltering heat, summertime was a most joyous time for that was when I was at my best, when my health was most optimal and it showed.

Winter, Spring, Summer, Fall

Fall characterized yet another phase of the seasons of change, and while harvest took place and knowledge continued to form, the reality was that summer had come to an end and it was now time to focus.

Summertime had allowed my light to be rekindled and allowed me to get ready to fight the enemy that sought to keep me discouraged, disengaged, and depressed. I was set free, and my character had matured – wisdom had been gained. I became more comfortable in welcoming this lifetime of learning for a sense of fulfilment had been bestowed upon me.

These seasons of faith's perfections have strengthened me and, furthermore, have allowed me to gain courage and persevere with any situation when the odds were stacked against me. I have often been told that there's a calm after the storm, and it is finally beginning to feel as if things are being knitted back together all in the name of restoration of my faith. I have grown, I have taken many risks, and change has presented itself in multiple forms in these seasons. Looking back at my life within the last few years, I have endured the most treacherous journey that I have ever had.

All these seasons have perfected my faith in some way, shape, or form for it has allowed me to believe that there are new starts to everything – from failure comes success and being able to experience optimal health is a gift.

CHANGE presents itself when least expected, but then restoration will come around full circle. This was a season of INSIGHT.

Reflection Response Exercise

As human beings, we are to a certain extent impatient and would rather see speedy results. However, what we fail to comprehend is that the questions we usually have are not always answered on our time. It is on our Heavenly Father's time. You've been presented with the opportunity to read about the importance of each season and what they signified for me.

Now it is your time to think of your favorite season.

Begin with the end in mind and move toward creating a working definition of what that particular season means for you – using your own words. Now, commence writing about the steps you have chosen when letting go and having to rely on your faith while you went through this particular season.

CANADA

Andrée Nicole's vast knowledge of women's issues is first hand because of her personal experiences. She is an Educator with a Master's in Education from the University of Toronto, specializing in Social Justice & Cultural Studies. She is the Founder and Executive Director of Andrée Nicole Inc., built to empower and created to inspire. She is also a Certified Life Coach, Motivational Speaker, and the author of two motivational books. Her latest addition, "Strides of Strength" is released in 2016. Family is everything to Andrée, for without them and their continuous support, this transition would not have been as easy.

www.myeyescanseeayearofreflectionandinsight.com
www.andreenicoleinc.com

CHAPTER 8 Jonathan Zhungu

Circumstances Cannot Determine One's Future

I have realized another facet of beauty that can come out of a woman when she arises from the depression and prostration in which circumstances have kept her from rising to a new life. This I have learned from the life story of a dear African who was willing to share her story with me.

She grew up in a rural area of what was known as Rhodesia, which is now Zimbabwe. The African community faced so many social challenges due to minority rule then. This put more pressure to the life of a girl child, forcing many of them to endure limited potential. She grew up in a family background that irritated her for family and society looked down upon her. The natural circumstance of her birth was poverty. She came from a very humble background. Poverty loamed large in her family of girls only. This meant being of an African origin where a girl child is looked down upon in terms of getting an education, she had to struggle to pull through the pessimist view held by the society that there is no point in educating a girl.

Her parents had to live with the humiliation of being a laughing stock of the community because they had given birth only to girls with no one to carry name of the family forward. As well, they faced the probability of having the girls endure more misery by having babies with men who would refuse responsibility. This woman grow up with the feeling of rejection because her parents were expecting a boy child after having two girls before her. This emotional hurt of rejection pushed her to reject the fact that her family background would determine her future life. There are people with similar circumstances of birth who have done otherwise. They allowed their circumstances to influence their willpower, and then have had their DREAMS crashed on the rocks of disappointment, failure, and setbacks.

This woman managed to qualify for her "O" Level through her father's support. After "O" Level, she did some temporary teaching at a very remote rural primary school in Zimbabwe. The experience of living in a remote part of the country, having to walk almost five kilometers to the nearest source of clean water to use in the house, and waking up around 2 am to get on the only bus to town on payday pushed her more to want to change her life and connect with her destiny. Nothing and no-one could stop her.

After one year of temporary teaching, she decided to pursue her dream by going to live in Harare City, where she took some secretary courses and at the same time wrote her "A" Level through distance education. All this she managed through the one year's savings from her teaching position. She had to stay with her elder sister and brother-in-law for the three years she was taking up her studies.

That spirit of rejection kept following her as after finishing her secretarial course because she could not find employment. She would wake up daily, pack her folder file filled with copies of CVs and certificates to drop at different Employment Agencies and companies with the great hope of being called for an interview, but it was not to be for almost a year. In spite of all these challenges, this woman refused to blame the situation on her family background to determine her future. Some in a similar situation might have said, "I am poor because my parents did not quite love me being a girl child." She says if you make excuses for being poor, your poverty cannot be excused. Remembering that one is responsible for what you give attention to; so it is unnecessary to blame your situation on anyone.

She turned the disappointments that came her way into an appointment with the Creator of the Universe, the one who says in Jeremiah 29:11 *"For I know the plans I have for you," declares the Lord, "plans to prosper you and not to harm you, plans to give you hope and a future."* This gave her energy to refuse any negative circumstance brought into her life to determine her future but to shine up the God given prosperity promised in Jeremiah 29.

After almost a year of looking for employment, she finally got a job at a Non-Governmental Organization working as an Administration Assistance. This enabled her to have the money to continue with her dream of furthering her studies when she enrolled with University of

South Africa distance education, studying towards a degree in Business Administration. Someone has said, *"The key to success is to focus our conscious mind on things we desire not things we fear."* This woman persevered by sharing her time with work and also pursuing her studies. This led her to sacrificing her social life in order to achieve her set goals. She devoted more time on her studies that even family and friends had to take a back seat in her life. She took the responsibility to guard and protect her potential. She used the little resources available to her to inspire herself to activate her dreams and reach her goals. She had to discipline herself so as to be successful in fulfilling her God-given potential because she was determined to maximize the potential within herself.

The pressure of seeing some of her age mates getting married could not detour her from focusing on her desired aspirations. Even age, for she was getting into her late twenties, could not stop her from continuing with her path of concentrating in her studies. Some of her relatives would tell her time was running out and if she continued with her path of forgoing all social life, she was bound to end up failing to get married. But all this could not move her from focusing and pursuing her goals.

She said the beauty of her life was the fact that she came to know and accept Christ Jesus as Lord of her life. He had helped her to accept life challenges and recognize that victory obtained through Christ was a time past, meaning it is a victory assured rather than despairing and blaming her situation on her family background. She began to be proud of her situation in order to feel Christ's victory over her circumstances. She became content with her situation, knowing that it was redeemable through Christ and that the redemption was a time-past one.

In her second year of studying, she suffered depression which led her to being sick and getting in and out of hospital most of the time. This affected her studies as she could not continue for almost six months. She had to take care of her health and because of the medical bills which needed to be settled, and having no energy to concentrate on her studies, she had to put everything on hold for a year. This led to some family members and friends coming to her and saying, "We told you so, that you are living a dangerous lifestyle."

Inside herself, she knew the primary principle in cultivating one's life for maximum living is to destroy ignorance by the pursuit of knowledge, wisdom, and understanding. After that year of rest and recovering her health, she continued her studies with more vigor and determination to finish her degree program. By the end of the fifth year of study, she finished her degree program and graduated.

God continues to favor her as she now works for one of the big International Organizations away from her home country. She is happily married with two kids but still pursuing further studies as she wants to get to the highest level of education in her chosen area of study. She says nobody is too good or too bad to qualify for God's grace, as it was possible for her to sit and begin to make excuses for her situation, but she never did that. She joined the few who are committed to attaining their full potential by endeavoring to maximize their abilities.

Unlimited potential screams for release in the soul of whoever is willing to take action. This woman did not let the following determine or limit her potential: fear, discouragement, procrastination, past failures, opinions of others, distractions, tradition, wrong environment, comparison, opposition, or society's pressure.

She recognized what she is today is a product of the conviction that victory through Christ is victory indeed. Through her story I have come to an understanding that the circumstances a woman might face in life do not determine what can become of her future. The choice is hers, and yours. You are responsible to understand, release, and maximize your potential.

SOUTH AFRICA

Jonathan Kudakwashe Zhungu studied Bookkeeping & Accounts; he has always enjoyed business related fields. He also studied salesmanship. He later worked in a clothing store for five years. In 2012, he migrated to South Africa where he is currently lives with his family. He did pastoral studies at Faith World Bible College and has great zeal for things of the Lord Jesus Christ. He currently involved in Multi-Level Marketing, which gives him freedom to help others gain financial independence with Network Marketing. He looks forward to writing his own book soon. He enjoys sports activities, helping others, and attending business seminars.

Email: jkudak@yahoo.com
https://www.facebook.com/jonathan.zhungu

Individuality

CHAPTER 9   Margareth Nyakambangwe

My Precious Hand Bag

My story is about a beautiful soul, a beautiful mother with a heart of gold. I cherished my mother and l loved her to the moon and back. She was my mother, my Life Coach, my mentor, confidante, best friend, aunt, grandma, and above all my Hand Bag. My mother's death in June 2007 was a big blow in my life; I just felt my whole world had crushed, and that it was the end of an era in my life. A piece of my life disappeared from me, which left me angry, confused, devastated, and very lonely. I was left with no one to share my success or sorrows with. She was my everything! I lost half of me. It was too soon to lose her, but I had no control, it was fate.

She was my hand bag because she was always in my heart each and every day and she contained everything ready for me. If I needed anything, she was just there for me. If I had any questions, any worries, or fears, she was there to comfort, reassure me, and pray for me. I shared the matters of my heart with her and vice versa. She provided me with wisdom, knowledge, life coaching, ideas, life skills, the list is endless. I call her my hand bag because not a day passed without seeing her or talking to her on the phone. Just like the hand bag or wallet, you will not leave it anywhere. It is always with you, and you get all you want from it, be it your mobile phones, bank cards, money, identity cards, really everything important to you. She was there for everyone, not just me alone.

The death of a loved one is a life-altering event and life is not the same after someone you love is dead. I remember the day I received the phone call that she was gone. I was about to go to work. I just collapsed onto the sofa and I cried the whole night. I was alone. In the morning I gathered myself up and started preparing for the journey to go and pay my last respects, and to say farewell to a great woman, a great mother. She had always taught me to be strong in any situation. I learnt that death of a mother is the first misery or sorrow that a child weeps without her. When she was alive, I would cry with her and she would wipe my tears and comfort me, but on this fateful day, I was alone and she was gone. It was a terrible feeling and I do not wish to travel in that path again, but as we all know, death is part of our lives. Once you are born, the next thing is to grow, enjoy life as you live, and the end is death. Death is something that you never get familiar with. Every time it strikes, it leaves us heartbroken, lonely, sad, with so many questions, and it takes time to heal the broken heart.

She used to look after so many disadvantaged people in the community, from children, to adults, the vulnerable, and the homeless. It was also her part of work as a social welfare officer. This was not just work for her; it was her life as she often brought her work home, and work followed her home too. People would come home for her help at any time. She had no day off. She coached many women to become self-reliant and financially independent. For her, the sky was the limit. At the time of her death she was studying for a Sports Diploma, and she had a vision of starting a Sports Academy.

I had no one to help me go through the grieving process as I was far from most of my relatives. This resulted in me losing weight drastically. I really neglected myself. I did not care for anything at all. I was now living in my own world. I used to find it difficult, especially if someone asked me about my mother or if I heard people talk about their mother. I cried myself to sleep for a long time.

I did not stop going to church as I used to occupy myself in worshipping, but I did not get much help from those around me in church, hence it took me a long time to accept my mother's death. One day a friend of mine was bold enough to talk to me. I used to make it hard for people to talk to me about my mother; I would quickly change the subject. "I would rather not talk about it", I often said. On that particular day, I was at work with my friend and it was just the two of us. She just said to me, "Marge, listen to me. I know you do not want to talk about it. Have you looked at yourself lately in the mirror?" I answered her that I did look at my reflection every day. She summoned me to take a look at myself in the mirror which was mounted above the hand basin. I literally did what she instructed me to do; alas I was shocked with what I saw. I was now a moving skeleton. I was scared with what I saw – my own image. She sat me down and spoke with me. She reminded me of my children, that I was still a mother, and they needed me most.

After work I went home, reflected on my life and what I had seen in the mirror, and the conversation I had earlier on with my friend. I knelt down and I prayed, asking God to help me go through the grieving process so that I could celebrate the precious moments I had with my mother. At that moment I sort of heard my mother saying, "If it has not happened to you, who do you think it should happen to?" That is when my life changed. I started reading my bible again with a renewed mind. I had to teach myself again to revert my mind from the negative thoughts that were bothering me every day to positive thoughts. It was difficult, but with the help from my friend I pulled through. Every time I was down, her words would come into my mind and I would change my thoughts. Though in the process, I could still encounter people who would remind me of my sorrow of living in a nightmare for years. I was in denial for the longest time.

I give credit to my friend for she made me see a clear picture. She helped me to accept the death of my mother, to start celebrating her life, and cherishing the memories and the legacy she left behind. She reminded me that my children also needed me as their mother and I should be there for them or else they were going to lose me the way I was. Throughout the years, I have learnt that grieving is a process and one has to go through it. One might need professional help because you can end up with terrible health conditions like depression, high blood pressure, heart problems, anxiety, or depression just to name a few. If not careful, one can end up being anti-social because at times you don't interact with others due to fear of being reminded about the death of your loved one. One needs to socialize, but you need the correct people.

I learnt a lot about grieving or mourning of which I am going to share some of the ideas with you, the reader. One day it might help you, or it resonates with what you once experienced. Loss of a loved one, be it a mother, father, son, daughter, grand parent, best friend, or any close relation is a devastating experience. Let those who are mourning or grieving cry it out. Do not teach them because they are going through a lot. What they need is support. At times, asking them will help and just being with them helps as well. The heart needs to heal first. Be kind, be patient, pray with them, and thank God all the way. It is quite acceptable to let one cry if they need to, though it should not be for long periods or even months.

When you are helping those who are grieving, show your love. Do not judge them and let Jesus Christ fix them because death leaves a heartache and only God can heal it. Have compassion, and let your words be filled with grace and love. Listen to what they say and speak words of comfort. Reassure them if necessary. If you notice that someone is getting worse and deteriorating, refer them to their doctor, pastor or counselor; whoever is appropriate. I have also learnt that there is no right or wrong way to grieve or mourn. Death is not the only cause of grief, other distressing situations such as divorce, loss of a job, loss of property, retirement, major trauma, accident, or terminal illness can also contribute. Grieving is different with each individual; it all depends on one's faith, coping mechanisms, and character. One can also join a support group. It often helps to meet and talk to people who are in the same situation as they are. In most cases, your faith helps if you have a church joining into some activities. Meditating on the word of God helps a lot of people.

As for me, I resorted to my faith at the end and I found solace at the time of my grief. I found out that meditating on the word of God daily and praying gave me peace and it helped me to accept the death of my mother. Now I can talk about it. Before I could not talk or even think about it; I would cry at all times if I thought of her. Now I have a Foundation Trust in memory of my mother, carrying out the projects she used to do during her time. Jesus Christ helped me to heal my wounded heart. Meditating on Psalm 23 helped me a lot.

In the process of grieving, you need to do justice to yourself. Grieve with hope and do not neglect oneself. Look after yourself, try and eat properly, read a lot or meet up with friends, maybe have night outs, day trips, or weekends away. Show your feelings. There is no formula in grieving, but if you bottle up your emotions, it will cause further problems if they manifest at a later date. Healing a wounded or broken heart takes time but with good support and help, one will manage. The main aim is to be able to celebrate the life of the deceased and be able to carry on the legacy left behind. Another thing that seems to help is to have Foundation Trusts or Charities in memory of the deceased either doing what they loved or helping those who will be suffering with conditions similar to the deceased. It could be in research or offering support.

Life is a journey only when you take its route. You will then understand and will be able to help others on this journey or those who have gone through what you have experienced. Experience is the best teacher. I hope that my story will help someone out there. God bless you.

UNITED KINGDOM

Margareth Nyakambangwe is an R.N., specializing in Ophthalmic Nursing. She has vast experience in Emergency Nursing, and has worked in several hospitals across UK. She is a life coach, mentor, spiritualist, entrepreneur, and an independent beauty consultant. She is the CEO and Owner of the Alice Mambinge Foundation, and a philanthropist highly inspired by her late mother, Alice. Margareth is committed to helping the young, talented, and under-privileged children to achieve their ambitions. She is a mother of two boys, and a friend to many. When not working on her projects, she enjoys voluntary work, reading, traveling, cooking, and baking.

akmambinge@gmail.com
twitter@magnum2tj

CHAPTER 10   Debra Mowlem

Little Girl, Grown

There was a little girl who lived in a particular village somewhere in Africa. She was kind of a loner and didn't like to mix with other children. One would always find her sitting by herself, drifting in day dream. Carol wore a face of a thinker and seemed to be assessing situations and wondering about the "what ifs" scenarios. "Carol always has her head in the clouds. I wonder what is going on in her mind?" her grandmother told anyone who cared to listen.

As she grew older, Carol saw all the injustices of girls being side-lined because their gender and inequitable expectations for them to marry, at an early age, men who worked in the cities. They would then leave their young wives who would have to build their own huts, take care of the family, and work in the fields. The stresses of motherhood, the harsh life of managing the homestead, and looking after livestock on their own caused the women to age before their time.

The little dreamer was in a fortunate position that her family was well enough and understood the value of teaching a girl child. *When girls learn, everyone benefits* was the way they thought. There was more to life than the hardships of her upbringing. Leaving her village was the first step of Carol seeing the world. They wanted that for their daughter, so Carol was taken to the city so she could get an education to have a better future and venture out into the world so she would experience how other people lived. The excitement of enrolling in High School and living in the city was one of Carol's dreams come true.

"I can't do this." Carol voiced her concerns to her grandmother in a moment of panic. "You can do this. The whole family is behind you and are giving you their full support," her grandmother assured her. "You don't understand grandma. This is what I've been dreaming about. But now I'm scared of venturing out into the unknown." She looked at her Nan with apprehension in her eyes. "Have you got some kind of disability?" Grandma asked. "Grandma what a silly question to ask. You know that I'm not disabled." She smiled fondly at her grandma. They had spoken about her leaving the village for months. Gran wanted the best for her. "No one is born with knowledge. You have to acquire it. There is no end to education. The whole of life, from the moment you are born until the time you die, is a process of learning. And you my girl are lucky to be escaping the harsh village life. Go out there, get an education, and better yourself." Gran reiterated how much she valued education.

This specific conversation has stayed with Carol, the little dreamer, all her life. She had a thirst for learning – nothing was too much or difficult for her. When she came last in English language at the end of first term, she realized that she had to learn harder and be more committed. The trick was in laying low and learning fast. From then on, she picked up on her grades and passed High School exams with flying colors. That is when she decided to look for work and found a job in the city.

She was astonished by all the different accents spoken by the people from all walks of life that inhabited the city. Young people spoke their own slang that adults didn't understand.

For an African girl, there is always pressure from family to get married at an early age so one is not left on the shelf. As a result, Carol had the same burdens put on her to get married early and start raising a family. She was soon a mother, but unfortunately the marriage ended in divorce. With a child to look after, she had to find creative ways to increase her knowledge so she could better her chances of a decent life for herself and her child.

Carol held down a job and worked up to eighteen hours a day, but she needed more. With some research, she found a niche in the market for foodstuffs which were scarce in her country. She set herself realistic goals which she could actually achieve and started a business importing goods from neighbouring countries to sell. The business was a huge success and the more it flourished, she was able to create jobs and employed around twenty people. It also gave her the capital to build her first house and the means to realize her dream of traveling to other African countries and learning about different cultures and how the people lived.

Carol grew into a woman who stayed a child at heart and the sense of adventure still burned strong. She harbored a childhood dream of traveling abroad to experience a completely different kind of life. Whenever she looked up in the sky and watch aeroplanes fly overhead, Carol told herself that it was only a matter of time before she was going to be a passenger on one of the planes, taking her to distant places. With resolve, Carol worked to achieve the goal of going abroad.

Having been colonized by the British, she regarded England as her motherland. This is where she came to settle. When she arrived in the UK, she realized that living in England was not a bed of roses. To be able to live a reasonably secure life style, she had to work hard and all hours of the day and night. Marriage wasn't in her plans, but it happened. As chance would have it, Carol met someone, fell in love, and got married. She had two more children, and with them came the weight gain and the constant struggle with trying to lose that extra weight. Let's face it, for a mum juggling a job, home, business, looking after children and a husband is a tall order. She found herself eating on the go with junk food being the easy option.

Working for other people and helping them to get wealthy undermined her business acumen. Being her own boss was a viable option. Together with her husband, they started their own successful company in software; design, development, and maintenance of software. The husband bought Carol out when they divorced. She paused to collect her thoughts. Surely there was another way! She'd always had a dream to one day escape the rat race, start her own business, become her own boss, and do something completely different. The future was waiting on her to realise her destiny and live the life she yearned for. As an empowered woman, she believed that business was a vehicle for change. And if she could help other women grow their own businesses, she would have achieved one of her goals.

You can take the girl from the village, but you can't take the village from the girl. It's in her genes. It defined who she is as a person. Carol did not forget that her upbringing was humble and simple. It served as the perfect foundation for all that she had and all she hoped to accomplish.

As a progressive woman, Carol enables, inspires, and supports women to achieve their full potential. She organizes networking, training, and discussion events to support whatever their ambitions are, and aims to empower women to become leaders in whatever role they take on in both their professional and personal lives. She encourages people not to let others determine their importance, worthiness, or capabilities, but instead shows them who they are.

Carol has been writing from a young age. Her active imagination had her dreaming all types of different worlds and creating storylines. But she never gave her stories to anyone to read. That changed in 2010 when she decided to give one of her manuscripts to an author friend she met in church to read. "Your story is amazing," her friend told her. "Do you really think so?" Carol didn't believe that she was a high calibre author. "I honestly do. You should get this book published," the friend told her. Upon hearing those words, a seed was sown in Carol's head. She did some research and her first book, *I Wonder*, was published by one of the big publishing houses.

Her fans followed her life story and wanted to know what happened in the end. To satisfy them, the trilogy about different stages of her life originating in the village in Africa, her days spent in the city, and her relocation to England was born. Carol didn't disappoint; she wrote the third book in two weeks. Amazing what one can achieve if they put their minds to it and focus. The books went on to be best-sellers. To date, Carol has written seven books. To improve the sales, she started her own Publishing company, and her books are now selling in both electronic and paperback form.

Carol is her own harshest critic. She is tougher on herself than anyone else, and fails to take into consideration points of views about herself from those around her. Not only has Carol been a wife and mother who had the responsibility of bringing up three children by herself whilst holding down jobs to support them, she is also a mentor and an entrepreneur which are achievements in their own right.

When she hit the age of forty, Carol decided it was time to re-evaluate what had transpired in her life so far. She looked back at her years from the age of eighteen to the present, and was not satisfied by her achievements to date. Carol drew an action plan for where she wanted to see herself in ten years' time, looked at her strengths, weaknesses, opportunities and threats, and made the necessary changes.

Carol stumbled on to online marketing. An idea of starting her own business gave her a buzz. She identified a dream job that matched her interests and paid the bills. Online marketing is advertising and promotional efforts that use the Web and email to drive direct sales via electronic commerce, in addition to sales leads from Web sites or emails. This is what Carol wanted to do. She joined the programme and started training same day; opening a whole new and exciting world for her. She makes a good income from the internet and has seen some returns from the money she paid setting up her business from her own website in the first few weeks.

This girl, now woman, does not worry about what people think and say about her. Carol is comfortable in her skin. She is aware that people affect others' lives by setting their own expectations for your performance, worthiness, and competence, then telling about these expectations using labels to describe us. For underpowered people, they become imprisoned by the labels that other have assigned to them. Those people end up lacking self-confidence because they believe in the expectations of others.

Carol's life has changed so much. Financially she is in a good place. She is happy her businesses are thriving and has prospects for bigger and better things happening every day. Carol views problems as challenges. The word "problem" is never part of her vocabulary. She views a problem as a drawback, a struggle, or an unstable situation. Her buzz word is "challenge" which she looks at as something positive like an opportunity, a task, or a dare. Obstacles are challenges to her.

Carol has gotten into the habit of dreaming big and has accomplished her goals. She tells women she mentors that if they dream big, the mind will put itself in a focused and positive state. Listening keeps one's mind open to others' wisdoms and outlooks on the world. Carol has achieved greater things than she ever imagined all those years back as a little dreamer in the village of her youth.

UNITED KINGDOM

Deborah Mowlem is a serial entrepreneur, a best-selling published author, a Business and Leadership Coach, and avid Speaker. She is also a certified Zumba trainer. Born in Zimbabwe, she worked in a bank and owned an import and export business before moving to the UK where she obtained qualifications in IT. She started a business with her then partner together in Software Engineering. Deborah is a mum to three girls, juggles home life and business life. Her passion is empowering women and bringing them together to rebuild and rethink their mission and goals. She seeks to inspire others to do the same.

admin@www.debbiemowlem.com
admin@www.byobfreeads.com

CHAPTER 11   Jossine Kaizirwe

Is Being Single a Curse?

I've read the passages in the Bible that explain the blessings for those who are single, and the blessing that singles can be in the Body of Christ. But why do I always feel that singleness is a curse?

Singleness to me is like a curse in my life because I so much would like to share my life with someone. Singleness comes in different forms and shapes. Some people are single by choice, some through divorce, and others through the death of a partner.

In all cultures, the normal thing for people is to get married and have family life. Marriage is a great thing and has wonderful benefits. However, I seem to be among the growing numbers of mature singles who, by some unknown force, end up living a single life. I have met rich, poor, educated, illiterate, big, small, ugly, and beautiful singles. And what they have in common is singleness. The stigma about mature individualism within my culture seems to be worsening. This defeats the message "free to be single". I would have assumed that this stigmatization was a thing of the past, especially in the 21st century.

It's just so difficult to be in my shoes. It takes courage to explain how it feels being unmarried at the ripe age of fifty-four. Nobody cares to understand what happened to make me end up on my own. I would like people hear me out as I explain what my life has been like. I also don't like being single and have struggled with multiple relationships.

We cannot deny that humans have desires that need to be fulfilled. The desires for companionship and sexual fulfilment are very normal, and they pull strongly at times. There are so many single people out there; both men and women who feel inadequate as they struggle to find partners. I wish I could go out there and announce to the world some of the challenges faced by singles to the whole world. I would love to lay bare what is in my heart and cauterize the deep emotionally wound festering within. Hopefully I can start healing.

I hope that by the time you finish reading my story you will have a true picture of how I feel inward and how it affects me on the outside. It's not by choice that I am unattached. I often feel that society looks at me differently and wonder if being single is a curse. The majority of married people don't want to be friends with singles. As a result, one loses childhood friends. I hope people see unmarried people as ordinary human beings and not outcasts. We deserve respect and dignity.

Being from Africa, the cultural expectations are for young people to get married and have a family. All I have ever dreamed of is being married. I know I would make the *perfect wife*. I would have loved to stay married. I tried a few times but for me, it didn't happen. Aunties and uncles are assigned to give the young people guidance of what was expected of them when they marry. It includes advice on how to be a good wives and husbands and moral values of our culture.

The whole family would look forward to the day their daughter or son gets married. It is still common practice in parts of Africa for the groom's family to pay bride price; an amount of money, property, or other form of wealth to the parents of the woman he is marrying. This is similar to the modern engagement ring except that the bride price goes to the bride's father and is usually just a token designed to bring the two families together.

I came from a middle class family where both my parents were nurses. They raised me and my siblings very well. Our home was in the affluent suburb of Waterfalls. We never lacked anything and we lived a happy life. There was always food on the table and clothes on our back. My parents were able to give us a good education and paid our school fees on time. Fortunately we all excelled in school, due to the extra lessons our parents provided for us. I completed my secondary school and passed with flying colors. I enrolled for a secretarial course and secured a job with the City Council Housing Department.

At the age of twenty, I met and got married to my husband who had returned from Mozambique, where he had been fighting the White Government of Ian Smith. My husband was involved in the fight for Zimbabwean Independence and had returned from Mozambique where he had a top job in the Army.

Before Linda was born, both my husband and I were very excited. We planned for our child and started buying baby clothes. We were blessed with a lovely daughter and named her Linda. We much treasured her so. I was euphoric and felt as if I had accomplished something in life. This was unmistakably the best point in my life. Everything felt right and life was good. We had a second home in the rural Mtoko. I had wonderful in-laws and felt like one of their daughters.

After three years of blissful marriage, my husband was involved in a car accident and died on the spot. At the age of twenty-four, I was left with a three-year-old child. I had lost the love of my life. My whole world crumbled in front of me. I had no control of what was happening from that moment onwards. I was in turmoil, wondering what my life was going to be like. We buried my husband in the Mtoko where he came from.

Life went on, but it was all pretence. I learnt to hide my emotions, my pain, and seemed strong to everybody around me. Deep down, I was lonely but I stopped searching for someone to erase my fears, the person who would wipe my tears. My daughter was a constant reminder of the responsibilities that lay ahead of me. I had to work hard and make sure that she had everything.

Unfortunately some things beyond our control happen sometimes. I met and fell in love with a guy who I thought was right for me and my daughter. I was lonely and didn't want to be single. He was a teacher and could provide for us. But it was never the same. I always compared him to my late husband. This new man was an alcoholic, but because I wanted to share his life, I went out drinking with him and wasted three years of my life. The marriage wasn't good and we divorced in 1987.

I thought I had to stay married because that was what society expected of me. I was frightened, weakened, and needed companionship. But real love evaded me – I went on to meet a crook, liar, and womanizer. I had a lot of sexual health problems and was always in the hospital. I miscarried a baby boy.

I was now in the mid 30's with two marriages under my belt. I wondered if there were any good men worthy of marriage out there. I was alone again. That was the beginning of what I call the curse of singleness. I wonder if myths about Christians and being single contribute to making women without a diamond ring on their left hand feel like misfits. I came to a conclusion that I was focusing on men and not on God. I needed to have a personal relationship with God.

Every affair tells a story which has something to do with the state of a relationship where betrayal takes place. What is truer than infidelity? I needed this man so much that I forgave his indiscretions. I got involved with a man who appeared to be a saint. He was working on diplomatic mission in Africa. Life seemed sweet. I thought my luck had changed. We had great times. Unbeknownst to me, this man had a wife in his country of origin. I got to know about the wife through a phone call. However, I still felt deeply for this man who was cheating on his wife with me. Once again, I got caught up with a man I knew was completely unattainable. The fear of being alone was terrifying. I was trapped in a dysfunctional loop by the paralyzing projection. At the end of his work contract, this man gave me some money to start my own business and then left. I never saw nor heard from him again.

I moved to a different country looking for love. I flew directly into the waiting arms of yet another man. I was not even aware of the pattern unfolding in my life. He paid bride price for me as was customary in my culture. They say lightning does not strike twice. This time around it did. My new husband died, making me a widow for the second time.

With the faith I had in God, I prayed for deliverance and God paved a way for me to come to the United Kingdom. I did agency work as a career and went to school at the same time. I took the opportunity of being here to get an education and make something of myself.

I am now fifty-four years old and less attractive. My body shape is not what it used to be. And even fewer men take a glance at me. Over the years, I convinced myself that I needed a man to complete me; I was making weak arguments peppered with delusion. Life went on, but it was all pretence. I learnt to hide my emotions, my pain, and seemed strong to everybody around me.

When my friends see me they think I'm content with being single. They seem envious of me because I'm unattached and footloose and fancy-free. They don't realize that I'm hurting inside. *If only they knew that the grass is not greener on the other side.* What they seem to forget is that life is a huge challenge. They don't understand that nothing can replace the feeling of companionship, love, and closeness. It offers opportunities for sharing and growth that no other relationship can equal.

I am writing this chapter for my friends and family so they would understand my feelings. I believe the world should be kind and not judge, because no one knows the story behind anyone else. There should be respect for others. If we can all empathize, the world would be a better place.

Love is a wonderful thing and it's nice to be loved. I miss my first husband and the closeness to his family. He was the only one I have ever loved and will never forget him. He occupies that special place in my heart that nothing can touch. I have told myself I do not need anyone else in my life and have now come to terms come with the fact that I can be on my own and am determined to be happy, no matter what. I have taken charge of my life and I'm content and satisfied without a man.

I am glad now things have shifted in my life and with prayer, I am happier. Yes, from time to time I will go through challenges, but I am never alone. Jesus Christ is saying unto us *"Come to me, all who are tired from carrying heavy loads and I will give you rest."* But in coming to him, people must take his yoke, and submit to his authority. I feel empowered through the word of the Lord.

UNITED KINGDOM

Jossine Kaizirwe is an author who also trains Health Care workers. Born and raised in Zimbabwe, she moved to the United Kingdom in the early 1990's. She is the CEO of Life Change Training & Home Care Ltd. Jossine, together with her well trained staff team, enjoys mixing with both the elderly and the young. Her vast experience enables her to give the best quality of care, and she continues to grow her business. Jossine volunteers for "Save the Children Africa"; writing her first solo book; and aspires to become a Life Coach and Speaker. **Jossine loves being a grandmother.**

www.lifechangehomecare.co.uk
linkdln: Jossine Kaizirwe@ linkdln

CHAPTER 12   Faith Ekperuoh

Back from Hell and Still Smelling like Roses!

From the humble beginnings of being born into a family where I was the sixth child in a family of seven, my father was in the military and my mother was a midwife. I spent most of my childhood and early adult life in Nigeria. My parents were very keen on giving me a good education. As a child I loved reading and writing. I wanted to get into the teaching profession which made my father proud.

When I was younger, I always sought my dad's approval, which meant everything to me. I felt that by earning his approval, I made him proud and happy. I did many things to make him take notice and I went out of my way to do things I thought would please him. And the only way to make him happy was to study hard and get good grades at school.

Losing a parent is one of the most difficult things in the world. Just as I was just finishing my secondary school, I lost my father due to ill health. After his burial, I still wanted to make him proud. So I applied for a place and gained admission into a Polytechnic, to study Business Administration.

Being raised by a military father who ran a house like the army, and being surrounded by my brothers made me a strong young woman. It went to reason that I had to have a strong man as my boyfriend. Subconsciously, I think I was looking for a father figure. I grew up into a fine African Queen who needed a strong King by her side.

My first love relationship was with a guy who was the press officer at the Polytechnic where I was a student. From the very beginning of our relationship, I experienced abuse. For control, it started with shouting at me. This escalated to physical abuse. After hitting me, he wanted to have sex, but he called it making love…like a reward for his bad behavior. It became a vicious cycle of abuse and making up. The violence became more intense and the cycles become more frequent. It was like one of those revolving door syndromes that goes round and round. It gradually broke my spirit. I couldn't live with the physical, emotional, and mental abuse anymore. I prayed to God for deliverance from the clutches of this abusive husband.

As it happened, an opportunity to come to the UK arose and I left Nigeria. At last I was free from my abusive husband. Or so I thought! A year later my husband joined me in UK. I became pregnant with my first child. And the dramas of my life unfolded in front of me, yet again. Unfortunately, it is believed that the man is never wrong and everything that goes amiss is the woman's fault. This gives men power over the women.

We had children together but it was a loveless marriage. My husband always reminded me that he was God's gift to me and I should be grateful that he was in my life. I bore my shame, was disgraced and humiliated in every way possible. One of the most significant things I remember was when I told him I was pregnant with my last child. He went into a rage and told me to go get rid of the baby because I was trying to tie him down.

One winter's night in December, without caring about the damage to the baby I was carrying, he beat me to a stage where I ran outside to seek safety with no shoes on and the temperature outside was -16 degrees Celsius.

I could not take this anymore. Boldness came over me. I went back to the house, straight to the kitchen, and took a knife from the drawer. My husband came into the kitchen and started to verbally abuse me. When he looked at me, he saw the knife in my hand and realized he was looking at a woman who had enough of the abuse and wasn't going to take any more.

I was a different person. I was not afraid. There was rage in my eyes and so much anger in me I began to shake. I was ready to use the knife on him if he as much as touched me one more time. This was the turning point. My abuser retreated to the other room. My father had sown the seeds of discipline, strength, courage, and focus. I looked at the knife in my hand and wondered what would have happened. In my eyes, it was self defence. It was either me or him.

Only God knows. The marriage was a sham. There really was no love lost between us. We had a strong hatred for one another. Both of us didn't attempt to conceal it. I had been sleeping with the devil and had children with him. My abuser always told me that he was a father. He was not intelligent enough to know that anybody can be father, but it takes someone special to be a Dad. This deadbeat father would take my children from me, and give them to his lovers to try and turn them against me.

The night my labor pains started, my eldest daughter was so scared and begged her father to stay at home with us. He sneered at her, put on his jacket, and walked of the house. I prayed to God to keep me safe through the night. In the morning, my children got ready and went to school. I sat indoors, languishing and in pain, yet my prayer was answered. When my sister called, I told her I was in labor and was on my own. She took a cab, came over, and we went to the hospital where I gave birth to a baby boy. My sister called my husband to tell him the good news, but he didn't want to know. I didn't want him to be there in the first place.

In a few days, I was discharged from the hospital and I went home to the abuser. The mental and physical abuse continued. I prayed to God for guidance and strength during difficult times. God is always here for us, to give us strength and lift our hearts when all seems hopeless.

I confided in my sister about what was happening in my home. Her response was, "You have tried to make the marriage work, but you can't make it better because this isn't your fault. You either continue to be the victim or you become a victor. Let today be the day you stop being a victim of your circumstances and start taking action towards the life you want."

I took a while to start thinking of a way out of the marriage. The question was how and when. But as time went by, God heard my cry (Genesis 16:13). The tables had turned and power had changed hands. When I told my brother that I wanted to leave my husband, he looked at me like I was something from another planet. "Is this the Faith I know talking, the wife of Adelwale and the mother of six kids," was his response. Being a man, he didn't understand. But only God knew what I was talking about.

Then one time, my husband was particularly nasty. The abuse was escalating. I reached breaking point and could no longer act the role of his wife anymore. Once I made up my mind to leave my abusive husband, I was no longer afraid. I saw the new me emerge from within, a stronger empowered woman. I believed God would give me wisdom and a sense of direction. I was inspired. When I told him I was leaving him and getting out of the marriage, he didn't believe me. I had said the exact same words so many times; he didn't think it would ever happen.

He had lost control over me, and I wanted out of the marriage. We lived in separate rooms for several months until he finally got the message and then he packed his stuff and left. I went for counseling which wasn't easy because it made me revisit the bad places I had been. The hardest part was telling somebody I didn't know things about my life. I was embarrassed and ashamed.

As I spoke about my aspirations, my family, and my expectations which had crumbled in my marriage, I began to heal. Holding onto the baggage from the past would hinder the healing process. The crux of the matter was forgiving the abuser who had broken my spirit. I felt it should be: *"An eye for an eye and a tooth for a tooth. But I say to you, do not resist an evildoer. But if anyone strikes you on the right cheek, turn the other also."* (Matthew 5:38-39)

I chose to forgive my abusive husband, but wondered if I would ever forget. I couldn't wallow in self-pity. I was desperately worried about the effect this was having on the children, although at the moment they are very well rounded and happy. Even now, I am dedicated to my children and strong enough to have bounced back from this abuse for many years, and in all other aspects of my life I am happy. Making any move, particularly when you have the welfare of vulnerable youngsters to consider, looks like a step into an abyss, but I know from grim experience that you can't change the status quo until you take that leap.

There is a reason why my mother chose the name "Faith" when she named me. The biblical name means belief in God and acceptance of God's will. Faith, hope, and charity are the three great Christian virtues. Faith is the substance of things hoped for, the evidence of things not seen. This was true to my situation.

To empower myself I went back to college and brushed up on my typing skills and shorthand and began working. I began the journey of rediscovering true self. I realized that if I wanted to fly in the sky, I needed to leave the earth. If I wanted to move forward, I needed to let go of the past because it would drag me down. Empowering myself was a simple matter of switching my perspective and choosing to believe that I was not powerless. Empowerment is the gift that keeps on giving, enabling one to enhance and further his or her personal development and achievement.

When I began to discover who I was and who I was meant to be, my confidence began to grow. As each day went by, I grew stronger and regained strength with each passing moment. I didn't let the sticks and stones thrown at me by my abuser destroy me. They became my building and stepping stones. These sticks and stones used to beat and suppress me, ironically made me who I am today.

Only when I mustered the courage to abandon the misplaced sense of security I got from sticking with the devil, I knew that I began to see limitless possibilities created by leaving him behind. I realized my own strength. I was not a helpless woman, but a strong mother who placed her destiny into her own hands. But through this all, my greatest joy was my strong belief in God and my children. The fighting spirit of a Warrior Queen was awakened. All this stemmed from looking for love in the wrong places.

The abuse and rejection were hard to deal with. They became the building tools to better my life. I am now a diamond, a star, a queen of my castle. I appreciate who I am. I've been to hell and back and am still smelling of roses.

UNITED KINGDOM

Faith Ekperuoh is originally from the Niger Delta, and resides in the UK. She is an aspiring entrepreneur, International author, and administrator. Faith, popularly known as "Dr. Love", is a rising relationship consultant. She is a Business Studies graduate, who studied both in the UK and Nigeria. For thirteen years, she has worked for the National Health Service in the management of the hospital endocrinology clinics. Faith is a beacon of hope for singles and couples who still believe in love, companionship, and marriage. She is the owner and CEO of Celestial Cupidating Among many things. She enjoys reading the Bible.

celestialcupidating@gmail.com
ccddating@yahoo.co.uk

CHAPTER 13   Dora Arabou

Removing Toxins from Your Life, Even Those Walking on Two Legs

A woman's hair is indeed her crowning Glory. Throughout history, in fairy tales and in legends, a woman's hair has been seen as a manifestation of her femininity and desirability. The Bible says: *But if a woman has long hair, it is her glory. For her hair is given to her for a covering.*

Many years ago, I saw a hair curling treatment in a magazine. I thought it would make me look fabulous. So I went to my hair salon to get it done. My hairdresser looked surprised at my unusual request. Ordinarily, "Just the ends please" were words she was used hearing from me. However, things did not quite work out the way I expected. Following a series of unfortunate events, including the use of toxic chemicals, I ended up looking as if I had just been electrocuted. My previously long healthy locks were damaged beyond repair. Every time I passed by a mirror or anything offering a reflection of the disaster on my head, I was in tears.

Memories of my hair's glorious past and creating negative scenarios for the future became my obsession. I couldn't focus on the here and now, accept that something had gone wrong, and should look on the positive and live with the situation.

I spent a lot of energy, time, and money using alternative treatments trying to rectify the mishap with the hope that my hair would get back to the state it always was, even though I was aware that what had happened was irreversible. I maniacally looked for hats, scarves, and bandanas to cover up for the next year or so. I didn't want to hear that the only option was to cut my hair really short to give it a break and time to grow. It sounded too radical for me as it was a huge change in my life. I never had short hair since I could remember. I ended up with very low self-esteem and redirected my focus on how to cover it up so people wouldn't notice what had happened.

I woke up one morning to a realization that I had wasted half a year of my life holding on to my damaged, embarrassing, and toxic hair, falsely believing that I could restore it back to what it once was. I should have embraced my short hair and taken time to check out various hair styles to find out how I could wear mine. Instead, I was held back by fear, lack of confidence, and motivation.

I walked to the hair salon and had my damaged hair cut off, leaving the rest very short. And as the locks fell to the floor, I felt elated and lighter. I looked at my face. It was a transformation – a dark cloud had been lifted from my shoulders, freeing my soul. The embarrassment and stress was swept away.

I believe that a lot of us have been through difficult times and have allowed "toxic" substances released from other people, society and their expectations, our own thoughts, our workplaces, and our families to slowly poison our existence, make us numb, and unable to initiate any change that will bring us closer to who we really are or wish to become.

As human beings we have basic rights to freedom, safety, dignity, and individuality. We owe it to ourselves to get away from situations that make us feel unsafe, trapped, disrespected, or unworthy. I agree that breaking free can be just as hard as putting up with a situation. The difference is that by putting up with it, you will never move on and improve the quality of your life. All the pain and the struggle would be for nothing.

Search inside your heart and mind and learn to redirect your energy to a different type of struggle – the one that takes you closer to who you really are, the dreams that you once had, the people that really matter to you, a career that is important to you, and to activities that are meaningful. In order to do this, one needs to disentangle themselves from people or situations that are as disempowering and controlling. Some bonds may seem difficult or impossible to untie, but the longer we expose ourselves to toxic environments, the more damage we do to our emotions.

We don't have to mend everything that doesn't work for us. But of course we try to see what went wrong. We give situations the benefit of the doubt, we give chances, and we try improvements. We're nice people after all and we want others to know that, and to like us, don't we? But let's first like and respect ourselves. Let's get the strength from the inside, from the self, from our spirit and soul, from the thoughts and activities that make us happy, from the struggle to achieve our own goals, and live our dreams. Only then we can be sure that the people who like and respect us, do so because of who we are, and not just because we fit into their values, their dreams, and their expectations.

Most of those who judge you for thinking and behaving differently to what is expected and considered to be moral, sensible, socially acceptable, and appropriate to the circumstances are the same ones who wish to have the courage to challenge and change their own lives. These people are not interested in your progress and your happiness. And they are everywhere: our families, colleagues, partners, bosses, friends, neighbors, relatives, authorities, and so on. It's just like the fat and toxins in our in our food. It's not easy to eliminate all those substances from your diet and it's even harder to eliminate all toxic people from your life. Learn to deal with them just like you would with an unhealthy meal.

When you start a new job with lots of enthusiasm, energy, and passion, you give it your all and get paid at the end of the month. You're able to sort out your commitments, go for a meal, buy a new pair of shoes, or help someone who is in need. It feels good, doesn't it? It's actually great and if you're fortunate, it will carry on like that. But what if it doesn't? What if a colleague, your employer, other agencies involved, or your role in this job is not what you expected? What if after you've given your best, the requirements of the job are not being met? Maybe you need to try harder, maybe you need more training, and maybe you need advice.

But there will be times when despite all of your efforts, your work is still not appreciated and gets undermined. You don't feel valued; you feel harassed and bullied and are forced to comply with unrealistic and irrational requests. You feel that the workplace is not a good place any more.

You can of course put more effort into it, comply with terms and conditions, rules and situations that you do not agree with and keep your mouth shut without challenging anything, so that you get to keep your job, suffer in silence and get your salary at the end of the month. So what happens now? You have the extra money to spend on that pair of shoes, a meal out, but you don't have the energy to do so, you are unmotivated, tired and emotionally drained.

Toxic people and environments slowly poison your body and your mind, just like drugs. They slowly work on your system and mess up your brain until you lose every motivation to challenge their functionality in your life, and you falsely believe that this is the only way things can go.

Most people have had toxic friends and partners in the past. These are the individuals who suck all your energy, positivity, kindness, and profit from your life. Such people live like parasites, drawing or draining from your emotional, environmental, and spiritual wealth; people who manipulate you subtly or openly in one way or another. They rob you of your individuality as you end up following their dreams, aspirations, and expectations. These people just use your need for contact, acceptance, and love and they make you believe that you are only worthy of these if you play with it on their terms.

All relationships need maintenance work from time to time. A total makeover may be necessary for you to live a fulfilled life. However, you need to set yourself a limit to the remedial works and stop investing time, energy, spirit, and resources on something that can just be replaced at the same emotional, physical, and financial cost and at just half of the level of grief.

Even if you think these people are so important to you that their approval is needed before you can move on or change your life, why don't you try surprising them by being open about what you really believe and what you really want. Their response may also surprise you as they may be willing to listen and understand what it is that you want and wish for you to be happy. In that case, it is highly likely that they will support you with whatever choices and changes you wish to make in your life, even if this is not in line with their own expectations. These people add value to your life and it is worth keeping them close.

Start with changes from within by trying to fight back those disturbing thoughts that keep saying to you, "I am not strong. I am not good looking. I am not assertive. There are no opportunities." Replace them with positive affirmations. Synchronize your mind to different wave lengths and choose the tunes that you want to play in your head. Take control of your thinking. Train your brain to be open to thoughts such as, "I am looking for the strength in me. I am looking after myself. I build on my skills and abilities and I start looking for opportunities." Don't worry if the old tape still plays in the background – it will take time for these little toxic voices to die out. Just ignore them; they cannot hurt you. This is just a first step before you move on. Start treating toxic people the same way. Move away from them – their annoying voices may still echo in the distance, but they can't hurt you. When you are aware of your worth and are strong and focused on your dream, you give them no chance to get close and distract you.

Think about what you want to change in your life to make you happier. But don't look to your partner, your job, your house, your friends, your country, your style, your health. Take control of your destiny and don't let other people's wishes, prejudices, expectations, ambitions, bitterness, frustrations, and lack of motivation influence your thinking and behavior.

Be honest and fair. You don't need the appreciation of everyone. Make sure that those who fail to appreciate and respect you for who you are, keep far enough away so that they're not able to cloud your judgment, distract you from your goal, and put you down. Be on your guard. If you're in doubt about people's intentions, it's probably better to keep your distance.

Do not invest everything if your heart is not there one hundred percent. Stressful situations change you and the more you get involved, the more you lose yourself in them.

UNITED KINGDOM

Dora Arabou studied Psychology at the American College of Greece and moved to the United Kingdom to do an MSc in Mental Health Studies at King's College London. She completed a post graduate Diploma in Psychology and a Certificate in Counselling at Thames Valley University. She later obtained a Project Management qualification and is currently working as a Manager in Social Care. She has gained experience within various educational, health, and social care settings. Dora is excited to be part of this project, hoping to inspire and encourage people to be in control of their lives.

Email: dora73arabou@gmail.com
https://www.facebook.com/dora.arabou

CHAPTER 14   Dorcas Marimo

I Overcame Being My Worst Enemy

When people see me today, they won't believe I'm the same person of many years ago who lived a defeated life because of a decision I made which was total disaster. I was deflated, powerless, hopeless, resentful, irritable, and frustrated. The very fabric of my life had been turned upside down emotionally. I truly hit rock bottom.

My marriage broke down and ended in divorce because I didn't recognize the warning signs that my marriage was in trouble and we needed help. It felt as if my marriage broke down without warning. Something that had started so beautifully had fallen apart and caused me so much heartache and emotional pain. Heartbreak is more than just an emotional defeat; to some the pain is very real. Losing my husband threw me into a type of withdrawal. I found it hard to function. I went through depression, lack of energy, and loss of appetite. I literary ached for my ex; I couldn't get him out of my head. To begin healing, I had to stop focusing on him because that would lead to rejection all over again. I needed to get back to me.

When my husband left our matrimonial home, I made one of the worst decisions of my life. I focused only on my children who were everything to me. What mattered most was making sure my children had food on the table, a roof over their heads, and their school fees were paid. I forgot all about ME. I totally blocked out how I truly felt about the break up. I didn't talk about how deeply hurt and lost I felt. I was numb inside. I shut myself from the outside world. Without realizing it, I had created this enemy within myself. There was so much negativity which enveloped me that I couldn't deal with my emotions. I felt more generalized pressure. It was as if my head was in a vice. I was convinced that I had failed as a wife and mother, and my children suffered as a result. They missed having a happy-go-lucky mother to give them those childhood memories they could treasure for life. Believe me, each and every day I regret not been strong enough to give them the happy childhood they so much deserved!

I lived in a community where people celebrated one's misfortune rather than one's achievement. A lot of things were said behind my back. I was self-conscious and worried about what other people thought of me. I found myself in a deep hole and a very dark place with no hope of getting out. It made me become more determined to live an isolated life and totally forgot that it was important to take care of myself in order to achieve the balance needed to be able to take care of others.

I stopped attending family and friends gatherings and taking phone calls. All I wanted was just to be alone in my home. Some of my friends and family turned their backs on me as they didn't know how to get through to me. At work, I fooled people by wearing a mask that always smiled. No one noticed how miserable I felt inside. Looking back, I was heading towards depression. Whenever people asked how I was doing, I told them that I was okay even though I wasn't. I yearned for someone to look me in the eye and recognize that I wasn't okay and to give me a hug!

It finally hit me that all these years I had been my own worst enemy with the way I chose to deal with the breakdown of my marriage and the subsequent divorce. Shutting myself off was not the answer. But then, I still didn't know how to step out of the miserable life I was living. I had disconnected from reality. Everyone is beset with demons. Things were particularly rough. It seemed as if the demons were winning. But as long as I was living and breathing, I was the victor. I was affected mentally, emotionally, physically, and financially. I nearly lost my home, but thanks to my brother who came to my rescue!

Gradually, I began to realize that my emotions were sending me a message and that I was the one who had to create my own opportunities and happiness. I could not change anything unless I accepted how my life had turned out. Knowing my own darkness was the best method for dealing with my situation. It was far better take things as they came along with fortitude and level-headedness. Even a happy life was not without a measure of darkness. The state of happiness would lose its meaning if it were not balanced by sadness.

The purpose of this life is not simply to endure it but to embrace and take the good and bad it has to offer as the experience of life's beauty.

I confided in my mother about my distress. She became my rock. Her love, guidance, and prayers were a source of consolation and showed me the way; I felt blessed. I began to heal and get stronger, and gradually let go of the negative feelings. I had a life to live and children to look after. My heart broke at what I was putting them through. I prayed to God that one day they will forgive me.

During those dark years when I lost myself, I wasn't a good mother, a supportive sister, auntie, and friend. I wanted to take them into the fold and show them how I appreciated who they are and how blessed I am to have them in my life. I started going to church. However, as a divorcee, the early stages of the Christian walk were fraught with negative judgement from some of the holier than thou art members of the congregation. I was thought of as less of a person. It wasn't my fault that my husband left. Widows received sympathy and were readily accepted. The reaction I got was devastating and demoralizing. I felt like hiding from everyone in the church.

I found the strength to stick with my convictions and going to church served my spiritual growth and healing. A happy person lives in a gracious state of being. I stopped holding a grudge against the negative people within the congregation. It would have had detrimental effects on my well-being, including increased depression, anxiety, and stress. It became easier to forgive and forget than to let negative feelings crowd out my positive emotions. When one is happy, everyone around them is happy.

In my prayers I sought the Lord and got to know Him. In return, He showed me unconditional love and that my marital status didn't matter to Him what challenges I faced. With Him in my life, I could overcome any trials and tribulations. I was the apple of His eye. It made me realize that life was too short and was to be enjoyed no matter what. I learned that I alone was responsible for my happiness; no one else. With a clearer head and new mind-set, I vowed to greet a new feeling of embracing happiness and empowerment. It brought to mind a quote by Lisa Nichols: "I am my own rescue." Only I, with the help of the Almighty, could rescue me.

It wasn't easy but I had to start examining myself in order to initiate the healing process. I started to get control of my life back. Reading the word of God and praying helped me to renew my mind and see things differently. I learned that shying away from life challenges was not the answer. It made matters worse. Pain, misery, and hurt can be gifts when dealt with properly as they make you stronger. At one stage or another, we all as human beings face trials and tribulations; no one is immune!

I got a job working nights so I could take my children to school and pick them up at the end of the day. My niece looked after them at night. It was agreed that my ex would pick them up on the weekends. During school holidays, they went to Africa to visit their grandmother from the father's side. This arrangement worked well and the children were happy and content.

It's never easy when a marriage or significant relationship ends. Whatever the reason for the split, and whether you wanted it or not, the breakup of a relationship can turn one's whole world upside down and trigger all sorts of painful and unsettling feelings. Venturing into the unknown was frightening. I felt sad, angry, frustrated, and confused. I was anxious about the future of my children.

How one reacts to a split is very important. There are plenty of things one can do to get through the difficult time and move on. One can even learn from the experience and grow into a stronger, wiser person. Sharing your feelings with trusted family and friends can help you get through that critical period of your life. There are many support groups where you can meet people in similar situations. Support from others is very important.

I decided against remarrying so as not to inconvenience my two children. I wanted them to grow up without being surrounded by drama and enable them achieve their dreams. I learned to give myself time to grieve for my loss in order to move on. I made a mistake by shutting down as I could have easily ended up in a mental institution. I also valued myself more as I learned not to worry about what other people said or thought about me. People had no clue what caused my marriage to breakdown. My life was my own, not theirs.

No matter how strong your sorrow, it won't last forever. Grieving is the essential part of the healing process. The pain of grief is actually what helps you let go of the old relationship and move on. No person goes into a marriage hoping one day they will divorce. I am not one to gloat; life is way too short for that drivel. But some of the people who relished in my misery are now divorced themselves. I've even had the opportunity to counsel them.

Life is a journey to be embraced and treasured. We all learn from past mistakes in order not to repeat them again. The road will get bumpy at times, and one should not hit the brakes all the time. Like a satellite navigator, recalculate and give yourself a better chance of reaching your destination.

At present, I'm not where I dreamt I would be. When I made my marriage vows, I had beautiful dreams running through my head like the wildest waterfall ever. It was like I was riding a roller coaster to infinite happiness. I learned that our lives are roller coasters. Each hill is different, some hills are the same, and others are completely unexpected. I now live my life trying to make it up with my family and friends, and in the process I help others to navigate the route to contentment.

They say nothing lasts forever. My dreams were shattered and disintegrated like early morning dew adorned in crystals being kissed by the golden rays of the rising sun sweeping across the landscape.

An empowered woman empowers others. I'm learning to inspire and motivate myself and really live up to my full potential so I can impact others positively, encourage others to strive for what they want, and help them to discover their full potential.

My desire is that on the day when I finally make the transition to be with the Lord, those I leave behind will describe me as the "best mother, sister, auntie, friend and mentor".

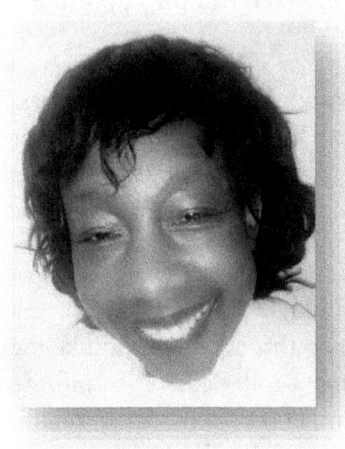

UNITED KINGDOM

Dorcas Marimo is a Registered General Nurse based in the UK with vast experience in both the private sector and National Health Service. She also studied Law at Anglian Ruskin University. In the past, Dorcas has been involved in various business projects both in the UK and Africa. She has dedicated her life to raising her two daughters in Essex, UK. Dorcas has a passion in empowering others achieve their goals. She wants to pursue a career in life coaching in order to positively influence and impact others. She also loves to travel and learn about other cultures.

Face Book: Empowered To Empower
Email: dmarimo2005@yahoo.co.uk

CHAPTER 15 Langton Wilsey Chibuwe

Her Labor of Love

It is not by accident that we are born. We were in God's care even before we were born. All of us are here for a reason. Some leave a mark that will be written in history. And others pass by without leaving as much as a blot on the landscape.

My mother, bless her, was not the luckiest of human beings to have graced the earth. But in my eyes, she was the most humble, loving, focused, and courageous mother, aunt, daughter, and sister ever. She was so beautiful, was slight in stature, and never put on any weight throughout her life.

She was born in 1940, in a remote village of Makusho in Nyanyadzi, Zimbabwe. She was the last of seven children. Unfortunately, she developed chronic asthma at an early age and it affected her rest of her life. She made the best of her illness and tried to live a normal life, with the aid of herbal medicines.

In most third world countries, sons take precedence over girls in education stakes. Her family was poor. They didn't have money to pay for her schooling past grade five. She was forced to live school at age eleven. The boys in her family got an education and one of them became a teacher. He went on to marry a teacher. When they started a family of their own, my mum became nanny to the children. She aspired for more and wanted to better herself, so she learnt crocheting and weaving sisal mats from other women in the village.

In 1964, she got pregnant hoping for marriage. But the guy left her holding the baby. She lived in a society that was so critical and judgmental; it shunned unmarried women. She forfeited the respect of her community and they would not accept her as one of them. She was called a whore and other nasty names. Her option was to move back to her parents' home with her baby with a hope they would take her under their wings.

With the help of her family, she raised her little boy God blessed her with. She was so artistic. She used her skills for crocheting table cloths, settee covers, and decorative items for the home and made a living selling them, continuing her quest for normalcy. All she ever wanted was to be a productive member of the community who commanded respect, and who was loved and accepted. Her hope was one day to find a man who would accept her child as his own and give her the sense of dignity and normality she lost.

In 1967 she met another guy and fell in love. They say history repeats itself. She got pregnant again and had another little baby boy outside of wedlock. And the unforgiving community piled on the disapproval.

And then in 1970, she got pregnant the third time. It seemed that she never learned from her previous mistakes. No wonder people believed she was possessed by some evil forces, or that people had put a curse on her. Imagine having three children with different fathers! What a stigma. She scandalized the sensibilities of her community. Her sons were not spared the prejudices and disrespect. They grew up with the stigma of not having a father to give them his name. It seemed children without fathers were cursed somehow and didn't deserve recognition as human beings, or attend school or church with everybody else with those who put themselves on a pedestal because they had what is termed "normal family unit" with mother, father, and children.

With three children to feed on her own, she supplemented her income by taking any jobs going from weeding, to harvesting crops, and tilling the land for very little pay. Even with a debilitating disease, she was not a quitter and was mentally strong, but physically weak. When she worked in the fields, her asthma got worse from pollen and dust. She coughed continuously and shortness of breathing disorder escalated. There were times she couldn't work and spent days recovering indoors.

The agricultural sector is by far the largest place where child labor is found. Her boys were assigned to herding livestock and working for others in the fields. They did menial jobs for other people and lived life in the periphery of normalcy.

Their mother knew the value of education. The only way to elevate the status of her boys was to give them secondary schooling and even apprenticeships to learn a trade. She had an ally in her brother and his wife who helped financially. The uncle took the role of a father figure to the boys. With the hard work and the exposure to harsh environmental conditions the asthma took hold. But she focused on giving her boys the best chance so they could be productive members of society. She worked extra hard to pay for their education. She wanted them to have their own families and be the responsible fathers their community would envy and admire.

She believed it was honorable to show true strength, respect, and understanding. With God's grace, she lived to see her boys become men who took their positions in the wider community. My eldest brother is a first class journeyman in the field of bricklaying. He worked in Botswana and South Africa, and in one of the largest construction companies. He made it his mission to leave his mark on some of the historic and prominent buildings in Zimbabwe.

The middle brother is a free spirited artist who uses paint and brush strokes to work wonders on canvas. His work takes him all over the country putting inscriptions and graphic designs on shop fronts and buildings.

My name is Langton, the baby of the family. I am one of the three little boys who were shunned by our village. But then, I became one of the success stories in my neighborhood. Thanks to the efforts of my dear mother.

I loved nothing better than working the land and watching fruits and vegetables grow. I was awarded a bursary to study Horticulture at Agricultural College. I studied in Europe and I've been to most parts of southern Africa and Asia. I worked for the Municipal council and was instrumental in the creation and maintenance of wonderful parks and gardens in the city.

When I graduated, mum traveled from Manicaland to the city to witness my achievements. It was validation that she had won the battle and had managed to give her sons better lives. But then a few months later, she succumbed to the asthma. As her sons, we know she died a happy woman.

We are still attached to our community. We let bygones be bygones and have no hard feelings. We realize it was the culture that perpetuated prejudice and was unforgiving. Yes, there are bad people who do terrible things and are not redeemable. But there are good people around. Like our mother, we are reluctant to give up on folks. To keep our mother's legacy going, we took over from where she left off. And we continue advising on the Home industries which are the financial lifeline of the community to this day. It provides scholarships for those who cannot afford to pay fees for their children.

All this is because of the determination of our mother, who despite all the torment she and her children suffered, she focused on the positive and worked towards improving her neighborhood. She gave us a lot of advice. The one which stuck with us till today is, *Failure is not a desired option. The harder you try, the closer you get to realizing your dreams.* She taught by example, and lived to see us grow up to become men who took their place in society. All of us are married and have our own children whom we are doing the best to support.

Mum was so proud of her boys. Whenever we managed to get together for family gatherings, her pride in us overflowed. She had achieved the near impossible by setting us for a better future. Apostle Paul said in 2 Timothy 4:7, *"I have fought a good fight, I have finished my course, I have kept the faith. I have finished the race"* Holman Christian Standard Bible. Rest in eternal peace; the epitome of a fighting mother.

I salute my mother. She fought against marginalization of women and girl children and was champion for Women's Rights and Empowerment of girls. She struggled with illness for close to half a century, but it didn't stop her quest for putting women's issues in the forefront so their lives are not blighted by hunger and strife. She believed that if people were valued, they had the potential to give something back to society.

Millions around the world live in poverty, simply because they are women. Their unequal position in society means they have less power, less money, no protection from violence, and no access to education and healthcare. Despite these injustices, women everywhere are standing up to claim their rights and fight poverty. Africa has a large quantity of natural resources including diamonds, salt, gold, iron, cobalt, uranium, copper, silver, petroleum, woods, and tropical fruits.

What people need to do is to be creative and think out of the box. People don't always need money to purchase some of the materials needed to make their lives easier. All they have to do is look around them and see the abundance of raw materials such as different colored soils for pottery or wood for building. After getting inspiration from magazines, she encouraged people to think out of the box. There were different types of grasses around that could be used for handmade table runners, place mats, natural rollable grass straw placemats, and table runners for the home. These would be sold in the cities.

There were acres of Aloe Vera succulent plant species which grew wild all around them that was used in herbal medicine. It could be harvested, stripped to make sisal for mats, rope for use around the homestead including tying up cattle when tilling the land and much more. Together with other women, they formed Cooperatives and started home industries for Handicrafts such as dressmaking, knitting, pottery, and building homes.

On a larger scale, they harvested, washed, decorticated sisal, and sold it for manufacture of agricultural twines and in craft paper production. They sold the raw materials for ropes, twines, and both low-cost and specialty paper, dartboards, buffing cloth, filters, geo-textiles, mattresses, carpets and wall coverings, handicrafts, and much more. This would command a significant price premium on the community.

Along the riverbeds people picked up beautifully shaped rocks and stones and sold them in the cities to decorate homes and gardens. Hot stones have a variety of uses. They can be heated up in the winter and used as bed warmers and for hot stone massage.

I am the proud product of my mother's foresight and hard work. She died without fully enjoying the fruits of her struggle. Even without education, she was a visionary.

I am married with my own family. My mother's teachings live with me. I instill them in my children, especially my daughters, to aspire to be great because society is against women and want to disempower them. Just because some of us live in societies that treat women as second class citizens, this is no reason why they shouldn't be forward thinking. Remember, single mothers can raise world changers. "Yes we can," were the wise words of President Obama.

God gives life to all mankind. He determines which race, tribe, community, and the woman and man best suited to be your parents. My mother was my mentor. She taught her boys many life lessons and to never give up on our dreams. We should fight for what we believe in.

ZIMBABWE

Langton Chibuwe is an International author and poet. He is a customer service trainer, and an environmental campaigner. After graduating in Horticulture in 1993, Langton worked as a horticulturist with the Harare municipality. He left Harare municipality in 2000 and went to study Information Systems with the Institute of the Management of Information Systems in the United Kingdom. He is currently organizing and establishing an environmental campaign to operate as an NGO in Zimbabwe. Langton enjoys taking part in community enhancing projects that help to alleviate poverty, and improve the livelihoods of vulnerable communities. Langton enjoys playing golf, pool, and watching environmental documentaries.

lwchibuwe@gmail.com
www.facebook.com/langtonwilseychibuwe

CHAPTER 16   Lynette Mutasa

Restoration of Hope

Rrrring. I was awoken by the school bell ringing, waking me up from my daydream. Day dreaming for a majority of people is what they do when they are bored, but for me it was where I lived most of the time. I had mastered the art of being there but not really being present. I had become so used to living my life in my head because at least there I could make the rules, I could be loved and accepted, but above all else I would be normal. Normal, that's a word you could never put in the same sentence as my name. I have always been outside of what the world deems normal. I am very loud and flamboyant, a little crazy, and very out there.

You see, only a few months away from being twenty-six, I stand at a wonderful four foot, nine inches. I would invite you to imagine how tiny I was as a small child. I was unable to start school at the normal age because of this very reason and whilst cousins and people my age were in school, I was at home. Those were the first signs to me that I wasn't normal. I was the only black pupil in my secondary school when my family moved to a small little town called Bideford in Devon, the lovely countryside in England. We were the only black family and there were two other black people in the town who had been adopted by a white family. Once again, I found myself not normal. Being from an African family in the western community was incredibly difficult. My mother was very strict and she so badly wanted to hold on to the African values of raising a girl child which in itself was not wrong but it caused friction with my life outside of the home. Whilst my friends met after school and socialized, I was not allowed and instead had to stay in the house to do housework and help take care of my brother and sister. Once again I found myself an outcast. My life in and out of the school was turbulent to say the least. I have been abused in every way you could imagine but it didn't matter to me because I had become so used to living in my daydreams and blocking out the world that no one ever knew what was really going on inside. I'm sure no one really cared because what I displayed outwardly was unusual enough. I was very ambitious and I always knew I was destined for greatness. I always spoke of my expected end. Even at a small age I would daydream about being wealthy and influential. I had a voice and I was very good with my words.

In my teens I met a boy who saw me for who I was. He was incredibly good-looking and he was so cool. He was mixed race, well known in our town, and he wasn't short of female attention, but he chose me! He saw past my hurt and pain and offered me a world I had only lived in my mind. For once I felt normal and needless to say I fell in love head first, no parachute and not looking back. Even the thought of it still warms my heart to this very day. I had found my savior and all was right with the world. Our relationship was a whirlwind and after two weeks I had moved in with him and his family. Slowly all my dreams started fading away when I became pregnant at seventeen whilst in college. My hopes of going to university were carefully folded away and I embarked on the journey of being a mother and being everything my beau needed me to be. It was the least I could do since he had saved me from the world. His character moulded mine and before I knew it, I was a completely different person. I had found friends who I could go out with and partying became the norm but not for long. My Prince Charming strayed…and again and again. My whole world was shattered and I had nowhere to turn. The one person who had made me feel normal wasn't there anymore. I had become what he desired for me, and to think that it wasn't good enough broke me. I had to stay with him and that wasn't optional. We tried, one more than the other I'm sure, but at nineteen, I found myself a single mother, estranged from my mother, fatherless and alone. The worst part wasn't that I was alone physically or emotionally because there was no one there for me, but that in my head I didn't know who I was. I had lost myself but did I ever really know myself?

I had recently connected with an aunt on my mother's side through social media and I went to visit her to escape from myself. She and her husband were churchgoers and they were active musicians in the church. Whilst I was there, I would go along with her not for any other reason than I didn't like being left behind. I attended a few services and found that it was fun. I got to dress up which is always a bonus for me, but one Sunday morning in April 2010 something changed. I was in church and the woman sitting in front of me turned round, knelt on her knees, and she started praying. As tears rolled down her eyes, I could tell she was asking for something from God and I was touched. She was a friend of my aunt's and I knew what she was going through, but out of respect for her and the intimate moment she shared with her Lord that day, I will not reveal it. I however was touched that she had someone to go to and cry to in her times of need. I can't be very sure of the moment I decided to believe in God but I would be confident to say that moment did it for me. I wanted someone to tell me who to become because I couldn't go back to the one who did not fit in. That was too painful. I threw myself into this newfound faith and after a series of events, I ended in the city of Cardiff in Wales, UK.

The beginning of a new chapter. I found a church and I quickly settled in, getting involved and making friends. Everyone was calm and there seemed to be a way one was required to act like whilst in church and of course I didn't fit this mould. Once again, I started not to feel normal. I made very good friends with a girl my age because we were both praying and believing God for a husband. She was quiet and graceful. She always seemed to know the right things to say and even in prayer she would pray calmly to The Lord. I wanted to be like her. I knew if I was like her, I would be more accepted in the church. I tried so hard but you can never completely change who you are. Fed up with living a lie, I slowly fell back into the world. At least they accepted me a little more than the church did. It was okay for me to be loud and flamboyant because everyone around me would be intoxicated, talking about the next time we were going to get drunk, or what happened the last time we got drunk. I knew in my heart that wasn't what I wanted for my life but it was all I had and I clung to it like a baby. Yeah, I was crazier than the rest but I was in good company. I moved away from church folk and turned my back on my faith. I had always been too worldly to be in the church and too churchy to be in the world, but in the world we could just laugh about how religious I was whereas the church wasn't so merciful. I even coined the nickname "Archbishop of Canterbury" because of how pious I was.

I didn't know this, but God was with me throughout all that. One day after coming from the club, I woke up early on a Saturday and I had a feeling to find a church conference. I looked online and I found a conference at a nearby church and I got dressed quickly and went. As soon as I went into that building, I felt the love of God and I knew I had to stay. I joined the church and started going every Sunday after coming from the club every Saturday. I loved church but I still needed to be accepted for who I was. This went on for about two years until one day I had enough and I knew the only way to get out of this vicious cycle was to find out who I was, and what this faith really meant to me.

I prayed on it and I realized the only way to find myself was to read the word of God. The bible made me stronger when I read from Colossians 1:15. It reassured me that Christ had the power to help me. In this, I had found my purpose even before I had found out who I was. If the word says I was created for Him, which means that I am to submit to Him. I am to be under his Lordship and if it was created through Him, then I had to have a part of Him in me. I had to ask myself painful questions. What is my character? What are my strengths and my weaknesses? And above all, am I ready to be who I am unapologetically? Psalm 139 became instrumental in rebuilding my confidence.

I now knew I existed for a greater purpose. These verses set me free. Not only was David acknowledging that God had him, but he was thanking God for making him who he had become. I began to embrace my negatives. I turned them into major positives. I started loving my height because I knew that just because I was short didn't take away from the powerful purpose God had put   inside of me. A bullet is so small, but it can cause great impact and I knew that The Lord would use me in the same way against the Kingdom of Darkness. Small as I am, God has put in me the dunamis power to destroy plans and purposes of the enemy. I started loving how loud I am because it just means I can praise the Lord a little louder than the whisper of lies the enemy so often tells me. Okay, people say I'm crazy but I say I'm passionate. I am so passionate about The Lord, and restoration of lost souls that I will do all I can according to God's will. I stand in good company as the bible says. Isaiah preached naked for three years (Isaiah 20:3). To me, that is passion. I have always been a black and white person and I struggled with that a lot until The Lord led me to Revelation 3:16, *"But since you are like lukewarm water, neither hot nor cold, I will spit you out of my mouth!"* Need I say more? The word of God has allowed me to be me and whom God made me. I can turn any of my weaknesses into strength through Jesus Christ. Whatever traits I have that are not of the Lord are prayerfully laid down at the   altar and I am free to celebrate who I am. My revelation of Jesus and what he did on the cross for me allows me to walk free of people's opinions and not to be kept bound by them. Do I walk around arrogantly? Absolutely not, but be rest assured the only one whose opinion really matters is my Savior's.

UNITED KINGDOM

Lynette Mutasa is the founder of a Women's Empowerment Ministry, Pumpkin112, which strives to share the love and grace of God through His undiluted word to the Esthers of our generation. An avid believer in missions, she carries the mantle of Love for a dying world. Lynette has an unquenchable passion and desire to see Jesus lifted up in every nation. Lynette is currently studying for a degree in Theology at the Bristol Baptist College and fellowships at the Newport City Church. She resides in Cardiff with her two beautiful children, Tyandi and Isaiah. She enjoys reading and teaching Bible lessons.

Pumpkin112ministries@yahoo.com

https://m.facebook.com/Pumpkin112-568355569997431/

CHAPTER 17   Sabinah Adewole

My Journey so Far

Individuality means different things to different people. I have come on a long journey, born in Britain into a family of four with one older sibling. I lost my Dad, when I was at age of four, through a ghastly car accident. We had to return to Africa – myself, my mother and brother, aged seven. Our lives changed instantly. My mother, a single parent, had to adjust to a new environment, having lived in the UK for twelve years. She was a secretary and had met my father, who was training to be a solicitor. I have no memory of my dad apart from pictures. With two young children under the age of eight, I often wonder how my mother managed at the time. She is my inspiration.

We traveled back to Nigeria in a ship. We had a bunk bed and I remember sleeping on the top bunk. The ship was moving from side to side and water splashed against the window. We were woken quite early for breakfast and would congregate for fire drills on the deck. This now reminds me of a very famous movie about a passenger ship. There were a bunch of children on the vessel, but I was not the social type and cannot remember making any friends. From that young age I had the mentality that I had to strive to win in life. I was determined to discover what was on other side.

Upon arrival in Nigeria, I was enrolled in a boarding school where I traveled three hours from the then capital of Lagos. In boarding school I met a lot of girls who had traveled from Lagos. I was in a foreign country having lived with nannies most of my life in the UK. I had failed to bond with my parents and I think it has had an impact on me. Sometimes I feel that people do not understand me. During the holidays I was sent to stay with family. I was not sure why this was the case, but I enjoyed those moments. I was able to form tight bonds with two of my cousins and we remained very close. I lost one of them recently to Kidney failure. My cousins have been quite instrumental in my life as they both went through tragic moments in life, but remained determined, focused, and never gave up. You have to live your dreams as no one will live them for you. My mother taught me to use my two hands and not to rely on anyone for my future. I can't say my upbringing was affluent but I stayed afloat and had to support my mother a lot and help her with her restaurant business.

After university, I secured a job in a bank where I worked for five years. I juggled my work and demanding domestic chores, which was hard, but I remained determined to succeed in life. My fiancée used to visit and help me with those tasks; he never gave up on me. We got married when I turned twenty-three, and later we moved back to the UK with our two sons.

Years ago I decided to set up an old girls' association following my time at boarding school after I realized most of us had moved to the UK. We had our first meeting in one of my husband's stores, and we had a good turnout. The aims of the group are to assist the school back in Nigeria with books, computers, and other equipment. We wanted to give back. Meetings were held regularly at each member's house. It was an opportunity to meet each other's children, create more bonds, and forge alliances. I was nominated to be the first president of the group. It was a good feeling that I was actually acknowledged for doing something creative and positive. We managed to send some computers and other learning materials to the school. The group has grown from strength to strength. In December 2015, we had a reunion after thirty years. I acknowledge that setting up that group made me find myself. You can achieve what you want in life using your own initiative and believing in yourself. Don't let others put you down. We raised £5000 during a fundraising event, and it is now recognized as a UK registered charity. Since then, I created another group for the careers in my night job. We had worked in this residential setting for years and never been out for a meal. I created a group chat and arranged a Christmas meal. We all went out and had lots of fun. Many joked, saying it felt like being released from prison. Most of the staff said this was the best thing they had done in ages, because they all had young children. They worked nights because of child care issues, leaving no time to socialize or relax. We regularly go on trips, including outings to theatres. The staff cannot thank me enough. I am grateful that I have this gift of bringing people together who form lasting relationships.

Human behavior is very fascinating to me. This has drawn me to studying Applied Psychology and I am writing my dissertation on

Personality. There are a number of factors that make us who we are. We need to find ourselves first; when that happens, you would know. Mindfulness has been my latest adventure, and my son got me a book on it for Christmas. I have not stopped reading it; it's kept by my bedside. I have learnt how to concentrate on the present, the here and now. I manage stress positively; in the past I suffered from panic attacks. This book has taught me how to focus on my breathing and relaxation.

I thrive most when I am doing something creative, and I think I have now found myself through the special grace of God. I completed my first book which is being published at the moment. It's entitled *My Story – Seven Years of Bondage. All That Glitters is Not Gold.*

UNITED KINGDOM

Sabinah Adewole "Koko Danielles" studied English Literature; she has always enjoyed reading novels from an early age. She migrated to England in 1995 and excelled in her career in the banking Industry, specializing in Marketing and Investments. She studied Social work and MSc in Applied Psychology. She intends to work as free-lance psychologist focusing mainly in understanding Human Behavior. This book is her first anthology to participate in. Her first book *Seven Years of Bondage* is being published soon and she has started writing her second entitled *The Fall of the Legend*. Sabinah enjoys yoga, Pilates, aerobics and cycling. In her spare time, she writes.

Email: sabinaha2001@yahoo.co.uk
https://www.facebook.com/sabinah.adewole

Personal Values

CHAPTER 18   Monica Kunzekweguta

Breaking the Bullying Cycle

Bullying has been a scourge of the playground, schools, and other environments throughout life. It has been against people who know each other and strangers since the dawn of time. It almost seems as a fact of life. Sometimes, many will gang up on the few for apparently no reason other than to inflict as much misery as possible. Sometimes the scars and memories remain and it may take more than time to shake them off.

I went to Mutambara Mission School to study A Level. I was really excited about starting secondary school. Having joined at the beginning of second semester in May, I knew I had to work extra hard because, as well as missing a term of learning, the school offered different subjects from my previous school.

I was focused on learning and did so well in my studies that one of the teachers used my essays as examples of expected achievements to encourage his students. But that didn't go down well with them since I was in the lower sixth "A" level.

At the end of each semester, it was customary to select new students' reps for the following year. Considering I had only been there a few months, it never crossed my mind that I would be one of those selected to the higher position of Head Girl. This didn't go down well with some of the students who had been at the school since first grade, and those who believed that it was their birth right because it was their home land. They simply assumed that the position would automatically be theirs.

That is when bullying started in earnest. Before that, it had been subtle and was mostly petty jealousies related to my achievements. This became orchestrated scenarios with both girls and boys, in higher and lower classes, ganging up against me. I felt as if I was surrounded by really bad Karma, and that God was punishing me for running away from home to avoid being a child bride.

It came to my attention that a girl from my previous school, Hartzell, was the one spreading gossip about me. I was angry at the thought; a lot of people were influenced by this girl's perception and portrayal of me which was completely wrong. I wished people would take time to know me.

For the most part I ignored the snide remarks, the silent treatment, and the feeling of being isolated. I suffered in silence but loved learning and stayed focused on gaining knowledge. Gradually, some of the students saw through the lies and hate being perpetrated against me by this bully. They came over to apologize and make peace within themselves. It was all about people getting sucked into the Mob Culture rather than being individualistic, thinking for themselves, and making their own choices. From there on, I made friends. Some are still in my life to this day.

As Head Girl, I had an open door policy till 8:30 pm. This was to allow students to come to my room for whatever assistance they needed, such as daily school life that they had problems with.

One evening when I was studying for my final exams which we were sitting the following day, one of the girls who had befriended me came knocking at my door. She informed me that a group of girls were coming to beat me up because I was an achiever in class. I noticed that my two roommates had conveniently left so they would not be in the line of fire.

It was incredible that young girls could act like a pack of dogs and plan on attacking an innocent and defenseless person who lives amongst them. Dressed in black, the girls would arm themselves with rocks and pieces of wood, cut off the electricity supply from the generator and then come for me. Like a cornered animal, I was paralyzed by fright. My mind was racing. I couldn't leave my room. I was aware of the danger awaiting me outside. It was dark outside; I would not make it to the matron's apartment without being attacked by the girls outside.

So I stayed put and prayed for a miracle. As time went on I realized nothing was happening and I began to relax and look forward to day break so I could tell the Head of School and the Matron in the hope they would stamp out the bullying. But then, the miracle came in the form of the school night watchman. He called to let me know that he had foiled the plot to beat me up. The ring leader wrote a confession and she signed it. It guaranteed that I would not get harmed until I finished my schooling.

Years later, I arranged to meet with a friend at Harare City Centre. I stood at the corner of Union Avenue and First Street waiting for my friend. Coming towards me was an unkempt woman dressed in clothes that had seen better days. Her shoes had never been polished and were scuffed within an inch of their life. I was drawn to the fact that each step she took seemed to be a struggle. It was as if she had lost all energy and life was slowly ebbing away from her. Her whole posture and demeanor told a long story of desolation and struggle.

I felt so sorry for this woman walking towards me. I unzipped my handbag to get her a few coins for her. When I looked up I recognized her as the instigator of the hate and bullying I suffered at Boarding School. My heart missed a beat and adrenalin began to flow through me. My heart was pounding. I could even see the pulsating through my clothing. Funny how something that happened a long time ago can affect someone years later. Pain and suffering seemed to be etched into every wrinkle and every groove of her dark and worn out face and trapped in her brown eyes. She was a sorry sight to behold.

Just before our eyes collided, I made a split second decision, crossed the road, and stood on the other side watching her. I did not cross the road to avoid her but to spare her the pain of realizing that by trying to turn out my light all those years ago, she had actually turned her own. She was now in the darkest place ever. She was surrounded by bad karma. What goes around comes around.

I wasn't the one to kick her when she was down, or embarrass her by taking her back to the place that would bring back memories of the time when our paths had crossed; a place she would relive what bad things she had done to me during our school years. I didn't want to be close and personal to the evil she generated from the past. I did not feel the need to show her that I had truly been blessed.

The Devil was in the detail. She was damned to live in poverty. I was about to turn forty – the same age as her. But I looked younger. She looked about fifty-five years older. They say a person's skin tells a story; well our stories were too far apart. She looked like she had been to hell and back. I watched her from across the road as she walked past dragging her feet. She was deep in thought. I think she was operating in auto-pilot, completely unaware of her surroundings, and didn't notice me.

I was a well-bred woman, who looked classy and sophisticated. I was confident and loved and respected people. The bullying I suffered made me put the feelings and needs of other people before myself. I was guided by a deep moral foundation upon which I build my actions. And I seek to build and not destroy, and continue to learn throughout life.

As I stood there watching her, I felt the need to reach out to her. I wondered what I could do to help. I even wondered if my gesture would be well received. What emotions would go through her mind if she saw me and recognition set in? Would she be embarrassed, happy, angry, upset at being reminded of the past, or what? Would she appreciate my help or feel I was being flippant and showing her that I was a better person than her? Sometimes we place too much weight on past events and are afraid to reach out to those who wronged us in another life, and miss a chance to save a life.

I learnt a huge lesson that day because I have never stopped thinking about her. If only I had reached out to her, I may have been of some assistance and done well by my God. I wish I had gone to her, shook her hand, told her that I forgave her, and released her from the burden she may be carrying (if she even thought about what a nasty human being she had been as a young girl).

It's all about the choices we make. That day I could have been hostile and demanded to know why she had targeted me and turned other students against me. I hadn't done anything to her and had never met her until our paths crossed and our lives were linked together at Boarding School.

Some of the former students see me on Facebook and request to be friends on social media. I often wonder if they have any recollection of how their hate affected me and made my life a misery. Does what they did to me ever cross their minds? Maybe it does not matter anymore because we are all adults now. What advice do they tell their children about bullying?

Bulling is a serious matter! It happens in schools, in work places, in religious organizations, in family units; in fact it is rife in every sector of society. But each one of us can eradicate this by being aware of who we are.

A Cherokee legend goes: *We have two wolves within us, the good one and the bad one. A terrible fight is going on between two wolves. One is evil. He is anger, envy, sorrow, regret, greed, arrogance, self-pity, guilt, resentment, inferiority, lies, false pride, superiority, and ego.*

The other is good. He is joy, peace, love, hope, compassion, serenity, humility, kindness, benevolence, empathy, generosity, truth, and faith.

The same fight is going on in all of us.

It depends on which one we decide to nurture consciously. That is the one which will preside over the other.

Always remember that we are all connected from the source. Have you ever wondered why the gratification from being horrible to another doesn't last? Have you ever noticed that it doesn't take long to feel empty and self-loathing? The truth is, we cannot show compassion to others if we do not treat ourselves kindly. Connection is why we are here. Doing harm to another is doing harm to self. Those who bully others believe that being vulnerable is a weakness.

The Creator gave us these senses; let's use them to do well. They are expressed through a gentle touch, a compassionate look, a cheerful smile, an encouraging speech, and a grateful heart. These are things you can give away for free and still can get to keep. Practice gratitude, joy, and believe that you are perfect and enough.

Having been humbled by life experiences, I have learnt to cherish all these traits. As I go through life every day, I vow to consciously strive to bring out the best in others so that the best in me will also shine.

Bullying is just one of the symptoms of our inability to live together as a human race. I have made a conscious decision that my beauty as a woman should not come from any endowments in my physical being. Rather, it should come from a deeper place in my soul.

CANADA

Monica Kunzekweguta is a multiple best-selling International Co-Author. She is a Certified Life Coach, International Speaker, and Mastermind facilitator. She is the owner and founder of ACT TO GROW, a life coaching business. Additionally, she built a company called A Woman's Beauty: the name was inspired by the message in her book. Monica is Project Founder of Inspiration for Kids International, a charity which provides library books to children living in rural Zimbabwe. A Sociology graduate, who moved to the United Kingdom in 1994, Monica has worked there as a manager in the Mental Health sector for many years. Her resume includes several self-development and leadership courses, and uses her experiences in life to help others reach their potential.

https://www.facebook.com/monica.kunzekweguta
Email:monicasbookproject@gmail.com

CHAPTER 19   Emily Mapfuwa

A Woman Empowered

This is a true life story of faith and perseverance against incredible odds. It is an account so many African women have faced over the centuries as they grapple with African traditions which have marginalized and undermined women. This is an eye opener for everyone.

The sun rose sweetly in the east as Ruth got herself ready for the most joyous day of her life thus far! She was to get married to Joshua, her long-term childhood sweetheart. Like a dream coming true, Ruth could hardly believe it was happening. The villagers all got ready for the traditional ceremony and her father handed her over to her new husband. After a day of celebrations, Ruth and her husband were shown their new hut and in no time Ruth settled to making it a habitable home.

Before long she was pregnant with her first baby boy. She loved her son and doted on him daily. Joshua worked in the city but was home every month's end with all the delights from the city. So life went on. Ruth stayed in the village looking after the child, tilling the field and helping her in-laws. Soon they had a surprise of twin baby girls! Now Ruth and Joshua had to fend for three children. Her in-laws were supportive and gave her all the help she needed with the babies.

Now and again Joshua would complain about the tribal inequalities at his workplace in the city. He felt the recruitment practice was tribalistic and elitist. The process by which individuals were selected and assigned to strategic roles was based purely on their tribal background. The company he worked for was owned by a Kikuyu family businessman. Being a Luo, Joshua stood no chance. He was assigned all the menial and labor-intensive tasks whilst young Kikuyu men were given administrative roles and supervisory positions.

"It might be beneficial if you went to evening classes to do some courses." Ruth encouraged her husband. Joshua took his wife's advice and learned basic bookkeeping skills. Soon after, he applied for the relevant jobs and failed to get them. He felt he was discriminated against due to his tribal background. One of the posts he applied for was given to somebody who was less qualified and Joshua had actually trained. This elitist recruitment process caused disillusionment in the workplace and murmurings of dissatisfaction among the Luo workers who felt they were working hard and benefitted the business but without promotion.

They wanted their voices heard and organized a demonstration. One day, before dawn, they gathered outside the gates of the company. They refused to go inside the gates to work until they were assured better recognition, increased wages and work life balance, and an ethic of care. To their surprise, the police were called in and they fired teargas at the demonstrators. The men ran for cover and a riot ensued. Stones and bricks were thrown at police. The police retaliated by bashing the demonstrators with knobkerries.

Joshua was hit with such force that he staggered backwards and fell to the ground. His colleagues carried him and hid him in the nearby shrubs. Unbeknown to them, he had suffered a fractured skull and needed immediate attention. After the riots, his colleagues found him bleeding from his mouth and was choking. With no transportation, they carried him on their shoulders to the nearest clinic. Unfortunately, it was ill-equipped to treat head injuries and Joshua died that night.

Ruth was up early in the village as usual, lighting fires and cooking porridge for the children's breakfast. Suddenly she saw vehicle headlights coming towards their compound. "This is strange", she thought, but rushed indoors to awaken her father-in-law who went to meet the visitors at the gates the homestead. Instead of her father-in-law telling her the bad news, he summoned his wife over. They exchanged words and then the mother-in-law let out a long wail and fell to the ground! All Ruth heard were the words "My son, my son, my Joshua!" Ruth ran over to her mother-in-law. "Why are you calling Joshua's name? What has happened to him?" Ruth asked. But nobody was paying attention to her.

The driver drove into the homestead. He opened the boot of the car...and there was a wooden coffin. She instinctively knew that was her husband in the coffin. At that time, Ruth felt a part of herself die. Her future was suddenly bleak. Her husband was dead, she had three children, no financial stability, no one to provide for her and her kids, and most of all no protection from the oppressive African culture that came into play.

After the funeral, Ruth was summoned to a family meeting chaired and attended by male members of the family. "We have come to a decision about your future. What befell our son was no accident. If it had been an accident, he would not have been the only one to die at the riots. We believe you are a witch and you killed our son with your charms. You and your children are not wanted here!" They shouted at her. Her belongings were thrown out of her hut.

Ruth was so dumbstruck. She was in shock and unable to say a word! Traumatized, she needed shelter, and the love and care from her own family and clan. She gathered her belongings and fled to her own village with her children. The men in the family sat and listened to her story. The African custom's edict is that if bride price was paid, the children from that union belonged to the husband's clan. "Ruth you were married. These children belong to another clan. They are not welcome here. You can stay here but not the children. They must go back to their father's village," her people told her.

"They are my children! I can't let them go back. They could be killed!" The men in her family were not listening to her. After all, being a woman, she was classed as a second-class citizen.

"You can take them anywhere you like, but they can't stay here with you." She was allowed to stay only one night. Ruth was up at dawn the next morning and left with her children. Her mother advised Ruth to go to Nairobi to look for work so she could support her children and gave her the few pennies she had for a bus fare to the city.

Ruth arrived in Nairobi at night and she slept at the bus station with her children. The next morning she went to look for shelter where she could leave her children while she looked for a job. Ruth knew no one in the city. After speaking to some women in the markets they advised her to see the city council leaders for help. She was given directions to their offices. When she got there, she waited in the queue for what seemed like ages. When her turn came, she was asked to fill in a form. Ruth was illiterate and could not write. A translator who was allocated to her asked several questions and she explained her plight.

"You have been given stand number 6007 and the rent is $25 per month," she was told. She didn't understanding what the man meant and showed him all the money she had. He waved his hand. "You no pay this time, but after work starting you pay," he told her in pigeon English.

She was led to her stand with her children. There were people living in squalor with piles of rubbish everywhere. Ruth could not contain the stench in the air. Amongst all this, there were women sitting selling their wares amongst the rubbish. They finally arrived at an iron sheet shack equally surrounded by rubbish and unbearable stench. The man asked her to wait outside and he went in. When he came out, he beckoned her over and declared "Right madam, this is your new home. It is nice and clean enough!" Then he walked away with a handkerchief over his nose.

Ruth and her children's life in the largest slum in Nairobi, and the largest urban slum in Africa had begun! She could hardly believe the plight she was in. Not even the village where she came from compared to what was around her. She had been kicked out of her beloved clean village by kith and kin with no resources.

Ruth was in hell on earth but she had no choice but make the best of her life by creating a home in the middle of squalor. Her children could not bear their hellish surroundings. They wanted to go back to the village and they cried endlessly. "At least you have a roof over your heads and no death threats from your father's relatives," she told them.

With the soap she brought with her from the village, she cleaned the floors and washed the walls. She spread her mats on the floor. Next day, she was up at dawn to seek employment. After looking for days, she finally found a cleaning job in a hospital. She was able to pay rent and buy food with the little salary she got. Her wages were not enough to pay for her children's schooling. It broke her heart to see her children at home every day with no future plans and no prospects.

One Sunday, she was invited to a local church group. She joined the women's prayer team. They encouraged each other and Ruth's faith grew. For four years, Ruth worked hard every day but her paltry earnings were enough for rent and food.

One day Ruth's oldest son, who was nine years old, came running to her. "Mama, mama!" he cried. "There are people in the market square taking names of orphan children. Please come..." he continued. Ruth followed her son and came to face to face with a group of ladies who were offering people cold drinks to cool off in the blazing sun. The next day they came to her home. She was touched that these professionals would want to help a slum dweller like her. She learned that they were from a Non-Profit Organization called *Voice of The African Child*. They supported orphan and vulnerable children in African states through empowering communities by self-sustaining projects. They asked her questions about herself and her children and noted everything she told them down.

These people gave Ruth the most astonishing news. Not only where they going to put her children through education, they were also going to help identify a small holding for Ruth to farm and earn a better living. She was going to be moved from the slum! Her prayers were answered. Her joy was indescribable. After all the pain of losing her husband, and being made to leave her marital home as well as not being allowed to live in her own village with her children, there was a light at the end of the tunnel. Ruth's hell was finally drawing to an end.

She was moved to a small half acre holding thirty miles out of the city. Ruth set about clearing the land. *Voice of The African Child NGO* helped her hire farming equipment and a tractor to clear the bigger trees and bushes. They built her a three-roomed home with timber wood. Up until this time, Ruth has been growing crops to sell in the city. She was advised that once she started making good money, she would then take over the paying her children's school fees. The NGO will get another widow out of the slum.

Ruth has been truly empowered and her faith has grown. She now teaches other women in her community about the love of Christ and his unfaltering provision for those who call on his name including disempowered women.

UNITED KINGDOM

Emily Mapfuwa is an International Lawyer in Human Rights, focusing on Child Rights. Emily advocates for the eradication of child trafficking at the United Nations Human Rights Council in Geneva. Among her many, she also co-founded Voice of the African Child were she serves as CEO from 2009 to date. She is also CEO at Arise Africa, which advocates for socio-economic development. She obtained her LLM from the University of London; holds an MA in Theology from Wales because she believes the restoration of dignity to mankind is through Human Rights observance and the gospel. Currently Emily is a PHD candidate, and has authored papers and books on child rights.

Email: info@voiceoftheafricanchild.org
www.voiceoftheafricanchild.org

CHAPTER 20   Godknows Kudzanayi Mashaire

A Mother's Love

It is not very far from the truth to say every human being deserves a father to earn them an inheritance, a mother to wish them well, a lover to show the meaning of love and a child to live for. Many African traditions have inheritance passed from father to son. Some laws on inheritance and birth registration still disadvantage women, even though they are the backbones of African society and play an important role in creating a nation.

I am inspired greatly when I open the book of thoughts of my childhood memories and reflect on the times I spent in my mother's little house. Words cannot express the love, gratitude, and appreciation I have for the woman. Throughout my tender years, she had been an oasis of love, guidance, and a role model to me and my siblings. It was always going to be difficult for her to bring up three children on her own. The sacrifices she made and the obstacles she overcame to guarantee food on the table, clothes to put on, a safe home, basic education, and reinforcing the importance of working towards achieving a professional qualification is a beautiful testament to the triumph of her dedication, persistence, and resilience.

I would not have asked more from a single mother bringing up her children on a small wage she earned from her job as a nursing assistant at a rural clinic in the villages of Odzi in Manicaland province of Zimbabwe.

Her life indeed confirms that a woman's beauty is not only her physical appearance, but her inner qualities and the way she carries herself. She was a spiritual person who continued to deepen her relationship with the most High and who believed in manifestation of kindness through works. In my mother's house, attending church was mandatory and it was through church that I first learned the values of love, of compassion, concern for the welfare of others, and to take a leadership role in society.

A mother is the starting point of a person. For a man, it is the blueprint that will define how he presents himself, his honour for women, how to raise his own family, and interaction with the world in general.

I still remember my first days in school at Mount Zuma primary school just across the road from the rural clinic where my mother worked. Mother would routinely wake up at five in the morning, warm water on a fire and cook breakfast as I bathed, getting ready for school. It was her daily lectures on the importance of schooling that made me grow a lot of interest in learning, something that has helped me grow as a person today.

Mum would dress me up in khaki shorts and shirt, black socks and back shoes then have a cup of tea with two slices of buttered bread. This was a blessing as I would find out in school that most of my classmates could not afford that, being the children of small scale peasants around the area. Most of my classmates were always taken out of because of lack of money to pay fees, and used to walk seven kilometers every day with a pack of boiled maize seeds in one hand to be in time for class.

Malaria was a very common cause of illness and death in the area especially among children. There was still a significant number of people in the society who did not believe in modern medicine. They were influenced by the local tradition and religion and their children were at much higher risk of dying from malaria. Once or twice in a year, mother would keep a watch on me while I took tablets to battle malaria. Chloroquine tablets were the basic treatment that were widely available. They had a bitter taste which I hated a lot as a child. The way my mother worked with other professionals in the community to ensure some of those children received treatment despite the belief of the parents was a huge inspiration to me in my career as a medical professional today.

My younger sister and I were raised mostly by my mother. My father would turn up to see us for a weekend once in a year or so. Mother would then disclose to us that dad had been married to another woman when they met, and had six other children with his first wife. Mother always spoke highly of him, as she would with any other person including all of our relatives and these are some of the values that got engraved in me. The eldest of my half-brothers, named Webster, came to visit when I was seven and stayed with us for a week. He was doing his high school at the time and it was a big inspiration for me having him around.

My mother's guidance and culture of hard work brought me the focus on my learning and zeal to succeed in school. I had a huge heartbreak at the age of thirteen when on the first day of secondary education, I got turned away from a prestigious boarding school in the area, apparently because mum had missed the deadline of submission of birth certificate. It took a lot from my mother to encourage me to go to school again the next day back in our small rural school. I did, on the comfort I would get a better school as soon as a place became available.

The next year I moved out from my mother's house to attend Form 2, not at a boarding school I wished for but another secondary school at our new home, closer to my father's village. If I could turn back the hands of time, I would never have left the comfort and love of my mother's house, something that can only be understood backwards as you grow. However mother never failed to turn up every month to supply me with essentials and always her inspiration and support for the three years I lived there.

It was when I was in a Form 4 class that I heard the news of my father's death from some of my schoolmates who came from his home village. I had not seen my father in three years, having last seen him when he visited the clinic where my mother worked back in 1995 when I was doing Form 1. It was quite a lot to swallow for a sixteen-year-old: all loneliness as my mother worked more than two hundred kilometers away and had not gotten the news. Communication was difficult; mobile phones were not readily available at the time. Even though I wanted to attend the funeral, I did not know where my father lived, having never been there. Some of my school mates had to arrange to help me to get to where my father's funeral was being held. It was a blend of sadness, anger, and fear. Sadness because I was only sixteen-year-old and had just lost a father whom I barely knew. Anger because I felt let down by a man who I believed had not done enough in my life. Fear because the future was uncertain. I then visited my father's home for the first time at his death, meeting my half-brothers, cousins, and sisters. Attending my father's funeral helped release the tensions and allowed me to concentrate on school. Mother was always there to comfort, inspire, encourage, motivate, and to take the blame.

I had watched mother's health deteriorate over the years from a chronic illness, eventually losing the battle five months after my father's death. That was only a month away from my final secondary school exams. Thankfully I managed to pass my exams to pull along into college. It was through her life, her loving, and the way she had given everything for her family that gave me the strength, courage, audacity, and dignity to go on. There is no day in college life that I didn't draw inspiration from her life. Her battle with chronic disease and the suffering she endured has always been a great influence in my career choice to be a medical professional. The way she had taken care of her patients at the poor clinic made me want to excel in medical school and be a great doctor and professional, and an inspiration to do well.

During her days, mother had always emphasized the importance of extended family in our lives. That would then play an important role for me and my young sister after her death when I was only sixteen, and my younger sister only thirteen. From early childhood, it was a ritual every school holiday to leave home and visit a relative's family for the four week break. Whether it was to my mother's sister's family in the capital city Harare, or to another aunt a longer journey further north to Bulawayo, or to our grandmother's rural home, family union was always emphasized. This then ensured a near normal life after her passing. We were never alone.

Africa is generally known for strong family networks and it is lessons from my mother that has seen me become a passionate advocate for strong family links. A brother's child becomes your own; the same way you treat your child is the way you treat your sister's. Indeed, there is more evidence that children raised in connected and intact families have more likelihood of success in life.

There is a lot to learn and cherish from the short times I spend with my mother. Strength and determination are key components to success in life, but equally important is the presence of a supportive family, a warm home, and unwavering trust to bank on. These are values that are abundant in a mother and often taken for granted. Mothers are a vital part of society and lay a firm foundation that we all grow from, and as such, motherhood should be cherished, celebrated, and supported. Without women there are no mothers, without mothers there is no love, and without love there is no life.

Empowering women through education, equal rights, and an opportunity to earn a decent living is one of the most effective ways to empower a society. A woman's income is shared by the entire family, especially the children and unfortunately that cannot always be said about men. Educated and inspired women are able to make informed decisions on critical issues like healthcare, education, and even political and social issues that affect their families. It is through lack of education and enabling environment that women often become exposed to child marriage, forced marriage, and poor sexual health leading to increased exposure to sexually transmitted illnesses in Africa and other underdeveloped countries.

I have learned that the plight of single parents should not be ignored in society as they have to bear the brunt of raising families on their own. Growing up under the care of an outstanding single mother and then as an orphan raised the alarm bell in me for the need to stand up for universal healthcare and education. It was also through growing up at my mother's rural clinic that I appreciated the impact non-governmental and international organizations have. They uplift the lives of people through the supply of healthcare accessories such as mosquito nets, pesticides, and medications to fight malaria and other illnesses as well as basic foodstuff to help reduce the impact of malnutrition and famine in the disadvantaged communities. I find it difficult today to turn away from anybody asking for help or to ignore pleas on TV from organizations calling for donations

It is through my upbringing with my mother that I learned how important it is to work to inspire others, to encourage others, to uplift the lives of others. It is easy to blame that we are all born in different backgrounds, with different circumstances, and we have unique capabilities and diverse talents. Just because someone isn't the best at any particular thing, does not always mean they aren't putting forward an effort. It is always worthwhile to spare a minute to go an extra mile for others.

UNITED KINGDOM

Godknows Kudzanayi Mashaire, born on July 1st, 1982 is a medical doctor, Pan- Africanist, African consciousness activist and author. Born near the town of Rusape in Manicaland, province of Zimbabwe, he completed his high school at St Faith's mission. He then moved to the University of Zimbabwe where he studied for a Bachelors of Medicine and Bachelor of Surgery degrees. He worked as a medical doctor in Botswana before moving to the UK where he continued to practice as a medical doctor. He is involved in projects to help unite Africans living in Africa and the diaspora, as well as African consciousness work "to awaken the greatness in Africa". He is married and a father of two children.

Gkmashaire@gmail.com
https://m.facebook.com/kudzai.tigere.58?fref=nf&ref=m_notif&notif_t=like

CHAPTER 21   Sikumbuzo Thabethe

All about Me!

You can't fix yourself by breaking someone else.

"To hell with your moral judgement. Who cares whether what I am doing is right or wrong? It's a cruel world and it's survival of the fittest."

"Portia, I am not judging you. I am just trying to tell you things that my mother used to tell me. There is a natural law of life that egocentric people, who take pride in hurting other people, always end up broken ten times more! It's inevitable that's why it's a natural law," I explained.

"I don't care what your mum used to tell you! Every time you say something, you are like 'My mum, my mum!' You worship your mum and her non-existent laws!"

"Look Portia, I am talking about self-worth, personal pride, respect, compassion, and personal values that evoke inner beauty."

"I don't worship my mum, and it's not just her who thinks this way. It's impossible to build one's own happiness on the unhappiness of others. This perspective is at the heart of Buddhist teachings," I emphasized.

"I am not Buddhist," Portia retorted.

"Neither am I, but when I come across posters and famous quotations anywhere, I take a moment to reflect on them," I explained.

"That's you Siku. Because you are sad. You and me are different," Portia defended her ignorance.

"But do you realize you are taking part in destroying another woman, a sister?" I asked.

"Ricky's wife is not my sister. Everyone is responsible for their own happiness. In fact, is it my fault that his wife is fat and now Ricky doesn't love her anymore? He doesn't even sleep with his wife anymore!" she exclaimed.

"Look at this, look at all of this," she wriggled her body whilst her middle finger was directing me to her body features, which she thought were unique.

We were living in shared accommodation. Portia was my housemate. There was no doubt that she was pretty. She had a glimmering smile, teeth white as pearls and enough to make any man's heart turn. Of late, I had noticed that if there was an area in which a lot of women were either helpless victims or simply acted savagely whilst thwarting their own talks about empowerment, was in their relationship with men.

I decided to sit on her bed so that I could try and knock some sense into my friend's head. What prompted me to speak this time was when I saw that recently Portia had even posted pictures on Facebook of her and Ricky, parading romantically at the beach. The more I tried to ignore it, the more it bothered me. I was just annoyed by the fact that it's one thing to do something wrong but to post it publicly on social media and be proud, was not only inconsiderate and arrogant, but impertinent and outrageous.

"Portia, I know you are beautiful. You are slim and tall, but all this outward beauty should reflect in your soul. My question is when you first met Ricky, just by estimating his age, did you not say, "Wait a minute, I need to find out if this person is single or married?"

"I did, but Ricky told me he doesn't love his wife anymore and that he would leave his wife and children for me," she replied.

"But the point isn't what Ricky says, but to guard your heart against deception."

"My heart is guarded with love. The only problem we have is Ricky is scared that his children will be ill-treated by their mother, and they will be taken by social services if he divorces his wife."

"Have you been to his house to see for yourself?" I probed again.

"To see what? No, I don't need to. Do you know how scary and insane Ricky's wife is? She calls Ricky constantly when I'm with him and he doesn't even answer. The other day she called eighteen times and we both laughed at how crazy she is. All I know is Ricky loves me!" she exclaimed.

At this moment my ears could not believe what they were hearing, and they told my eyes to squint in order to help absorb the information. It was pathetic.

"How long have you been dating?" I shifted the conversation.

"Four Years," she replied.

"What's stopping him from marrying you then?" I asked again.

"Patience is a virtue," replied Portia.

Deep in my heart I wanted to scream out and say, "What's wrong with you "virtuous" woman? Stop painting someone white when they have already shown their true color."

"How old is Ricky's oldest child and how old is the youngest?"

"Thirteen, and the youngest is four," Portia replied.

"Let's try to follow this logically. If Ricky cares for his children and is afraid that they'll be neglected, it means he is going to stick around with his wife until the youngest is eighteen. In fact, if Ricky cared for his family, he wouldn't be here trying to create another. He would be at home supporting them emotionally, physically, and psychologically."

"We know what we are doing," she smiled.

"What are you doing? If I may ask?" I was numb with shock simply because she delivered that answer with great confidence. While I was still deep in contemplation, another question popped into my head. The answer I was expecting was that she knew what she was doing because Ricky was wasting her life.

"Siku. You wouldn't understand," Portia broke the silence. "I am in love, and every time, Ricky talks about his wife, he ends up crying. Men don't cry, even at funerals. Ricky is a victim. The wife bullies Ricky. She demands his pay slips and takes all of Ricky's money!" Portia clarified.

I wanted to scream and answer that even crocodiles cry, but they cry tears of joy for their meat. I wanted to say that Ricky's wife is entitled to Ricky's wages because she has Ricky's children to feed, but I had also known from psychology that attacking a person whilst trying to advise them never solves the problem, but understanding them would. Tactically, I decided to move away from the attack side to a position where I could reason out the situation with her.

"Look here Siku, Ricky is not tied to his wife with a chain. All Ricky's wife needs to do is to wake up and smell the coffee," Portia explained.

While this conversation was going on, thoughts began to flood into my mind. Surely there was no coffee to smell here. What I could smell was a stench smell, indifferent wicked souls. How could Portia smile that she was participating in hurting another woman and actually enjoying every moment of it? Momentarily, another thought probed my brain and whispered, "Has Portia by herself woken up to smell 'the coffee of what exactly was going on?' What about the law of Karma, whereby what we do to others has a way of coming back to torment us?" I became biblical, "Love is kind. It does not envy. What had happened to souls? Love does not dishonor others, it is not self-seeking…Love does not delight in evil but rejoices with the truth. Love always protects" I Corinthians 13:4-8. How do we as women expect men to treat us better when we don't respect each other? We want them to fight our cause while we do nothing? Nevertheless, for the sake of a healthy conversation I kept my thoughts under lock and key.

"Besides, I am actually as good as married to Ricky now. I am engaged and I am expecting," Portia proudly explained.

I was bewildered with confusion. How can Portia rejoice that she is engaged to a married man? Polygamy? What age of civilization was she living in? If a man was incapable of loving one wife, what made Portia think he was capable of loving two? While I was still deep in contemplation, other questions gushed into my head. "So this was going to be Ricky's seventh child? If Ricky didn't really love his six other children and stick up with them, what made Portia think this baby was extra special? Afraid of laying my thoughts in the open, I dismissed them and I switched back to the conversation. "Congratulations!" I exclaimed. "How old is baby?" I pretended to be excited.

"Five months and it's a boy! His name is Ricky Junior," Portia bragged.

I realized my excitement about the baby had not really paid off. It seemed I was sending mixed messages; seemingly I had lost the war. Momentarily, I broke the silence.

"Porsche, I am worried about you, especially with baby coming up. When I was younger, mum used to tell me that how a man treats others or how he treats his children is how he will end up treating you and your children in the long run. If he kicks his dog or if he beats his current wife, or cheat on his wife, it simply means he is abusive and from such, stay away."

"Ricky is very loving. The things he buys for me and my daughter. Look at this diamond ring. How dare you call him that?"

I realized I was talking to a dead end, and there was no point continuing with the conversation. Deep in my heart I was boiling. What if Ricky was simply abusing his wife and Portia at the same time and enjoying every minute of it? Just because Ricky had this bright side of him, buying flowers and presents, did not mean he didn't have a dark side. Following this closely, if I knew that a man was doing that for me, I would never want him around me and my children. It's as simple as that.

"Ricky is not abusive. He doesn't beat his wife," answered Portia.

"I told you, we know what we are doing and as soon as baby comes, Ricky is going move in with me." Portia had lightened her mood.

Days developed into weeks and weeks progressed into months and before long months had blossomed into years, but there was no Ricky moving in with Portia. Cold, sleepless, lonely nights of looking after baby followed. Eventually I heard that Ricky had secretly tried to grope Portia's daughter and that ended the relationship. Portia was now a single mother of two.

Portia was not alone, in this predicament neither was Ricky's wife. A lot of women fall into this trap. Every time I reflect on this story, I realize a woman's beauty is a concept that starts with women advocating for themselves and for one another.

Whilst we talk about men exploiting and abusing women, the question is: What are we doing to protect and respect each other, woman to woman? We cannot expect men to fight a cause which entirely sets them at an advantage. Fighting the exploitation of women by men should start with us women. The more we remain egocentric, the more men continue to abuse us and treat us like commodities that can be acquired in large numbers, resulting in a new form of polygamy where you don't necessarily have to live in the same house.

To some Ricky's out there, it's not until you have worked with victims of abuse and cheating that you realize the despair and anguish that is evident in the victims' eyes. Moreover, we cannot tackle the issue of "fatherless children" and broken hearts if we are active participants in wrecking homes. It's hypocrisy. Neither should we continue to get carried away by flowers, engagement rings, nor pregnancy without making sure that the circumstances are right.

To young girls, ideally, avoid men with a lot of baggage. You end up getting entangled for life.

To Ricky's wife, the only way to stop abuse is to stand up against it. Begging an abusive person to stop abuse, only perpetrates it.

UNITED KINGDOM

Sikumbuzo Thabethe is smart, talented, confident, and writes with artistic expression. Her passion about women's issues emanate from personal experiences, and studies in Women and Development at the University of Zimbabwe. She holds a BSc. Honours degree in Sociology and a postgraduate degree in Health and Social Policy. Sikumbuzo has a strong Christian background and spends her time being a wife and mother. She also coaches private students, and is currently working for Mission of Hope as a Collector of Humanitarian Aid. She is also currently working on a book entitled *The System Fails Us* and an anthology entitled *The Power of Decision Making*.

sikusimango@gmail.com
mbuzie@hotmail.co.uk

CHAPTER 22   Harold Sharara

A Woman's Beauty is the Depth of Her Soul

A quintessential woman, whom I refer endearingly to as Kuda, had patiently listened to my life story and the circumstances behind my divorce. Her name in Shona has a deep spiritual meaning: "The Will of The Lord". This phenomenal woman had managed to rescue me from the depth of the abyss that I had fallen into. Working patiently and meticulously with me, emotionally fragile as I was, she created a comfortable and serene atmosphere for this torn soul to open up again. This unparalleled attention she afforded me began that healing process which I so desperately needed, and which would eventually bring me back to my old unbruised self.

It was seven years ago in Ottawa, when I lay on the freezing road one Canadian winter morning. Shinbone protruding out of my leg, I wondered why no one was calling 9-1-1 for the paramedics to come to my assistance. My neighbor, who found me, rushed to call the ambulance as I was passing into shock. Up to this day I wish I had told him that I loved my kids, but as someone who had given up on his own in Jamaica many years before, I suspect he would have not understood my viewpoint as a divorced father. And certainly, he would be forgiven for not understanding. He had left his first wife and children, and had now re-married (to a good woman, I must say!) and life was now bliss. Some men find it easy to walk away from a woman. They would not think twice about it; even if it meant walking away from the children too. At that time it had not yet dawned on me that, if someone you cared about was prepared to leave you even if you had to spend all your life in a wheel chair, you were probably better off seeing the world from there. I was probably naïve, but I was determined to try my best to always be there for my little ones; after all, the girl was only nine, and the boy was just three.

Half-conscious, I could still make out the paramedics arriving. What efficiency! It took them less than ten minutes after I had fallen from the car and broken my leg. But I will never forget the anguish, the agony, the excruciating pain, and the loneliness! It made the ten minutes seem like an eternity. By the time the paramedics gave me the sedative, I must have been singing in "tongues". The shot was potent, so strong that the pain was immediately masked. Ten hours later, I woke up at the Ottawa General Hospital after an operation. The first thing I realized when I got my full consciousness was that my mobility was obviously compromised. I couldn't move my left leg. At that point, I also noticed the junior nurse who was attending to me. She had advised me then about the operation and the cast they had put on my leg. Oh, eureka moment! No wonder my leg was heavy to move. I got to know this young girl over the next few days as she tendered to my health needs. And as we would chat regularly, one day she blurted out words I will never forget. In a Kenyan-Canadian accent she had innocently advised me about my relationship status. "My brother, I saw your work ID's as I was putting away your clothes. If you don't mind me saying, I think a man of your accomplishments can still be happy. She continued, "Some of us African women tend to stray from the great values that raised us back home." Although I minded the intrusion, I still gave her a warm smile, but my lips would not render her any utterance. However these thoughts quickly rushed me back to the words of my Jamaican neighbor, when he had come to my assistance.

Even as I travel back to that painful memory many years later, I still have no harsh feelings towards the mother of my children. The good years spent together have a bearing on how I will always cherish her as a human being. Despite the negatives in the relationship, she gave me two of the most beautiful children ever. We are all imperfect! There are always reasons why people who initially want to conquer the world together, can end up not wanting to stay together. The young nurse from Kenya had however made a valid point, and I appreciated her comments. It would take several years, several separations, and several reunions before I would finally give up on that marriage. On that day, with the help of my children, I packed my suitcases into my car, and never turned back.

Over those years, we had both continued to have the occasional and momentary lapses in judgement. It would seem that we were both oblivious to the irreparable emotional damage that we had continually inflicted on each other. Consequently, the countless separations that we went through, and still managed to "reconcile", were part of an incredulous phenomenon. The only way to rationalize this phenomenon is to attribute it to wanting to be together for the sake of the children. However, in retrospect I am well aware that the genuine love that we had once shared had suffered a loss of affection many years before.

Six months before I finally left, while we were on separation, she had decided to move four thousand kilometers across the country with the children. At the time, this was a mutually agreeable and amicable situation; for now we could resume our lives separately. While communicating with the children, she and I found ourselves reconciling yet again. Before long, I was resigning from the best job I ever had in Canada, and on Christmas day, hardly four months after the move, she was picking me up from the Calgary airport. We still had not realized the essence of what a true marriage relationship was all about. Three months into moving in together, it was apparent that we had reached the limit. Eventually, I moved out, and this would be the beginning of a happier dispensation in my life.

This new era of my life however did not occur overnight. It would be a protracted episode through pain, loss of self-esteem, and self-destruction. As it happens, after a divorce from my marriage of sixteen years, I was extremely lonely and depressed. I was just starting to get familiar with this new city. I had no friends, I had lost my family, I had lost my job because I didn't care anymore, I had lost everything I had worked for. What does one do when they are losing equilibrium, when everything is seemingly falling apart? I owe a lot to one specific avenue of social media!

On a particular Saturday morning, months after the divorce, I ventured onto a social platform. I had the least inclination that this would be the best idea I had ever made in my entire life! As soon as I had logged in, I stumbled across a group chat initiated by a girl that I had always secretly admired from high school. I had never had the courage to intimate my feelings for her back then. But this time would be different! Instantly, I was telling myself, "Ok, come on now...don't fumble this one." Her post about the importance of taking risks in life had attracted a lot of responses, and everyone who had posted had commented in the affirmative. I decided to respond as an antagonist. I went ahead and argued for the risk-averse from an intellectual perspective. Lo and behold, that got her attention. From that point, everybody left us to duke it out. Before long, we had taken it to inboxing, phone texting, and eventually to talking. The rest is now history. But sometimes I reminisce about that gutsy move that would forever change my world, and I grin with a splendorous sense of achievement. I am thankful that I was blessed to eventually end up with the woman I am writing about. A beautiful woman whose authenticity is deeper than the Mariana Trench.

After our chance encounter on the internet, Kuda and I continued to talk. It did not take long before it became quite apparent to both, that we were developing a strong chemistry. I would find out her life story that I had never known all those years in high school. She had gone through a lot of suffering, narrowly escaping being given away as a child bride at fifteen. Later, in high school, she had been the victim of the harshest bullying imaginable. As she gave me an account of her life experiences, all I could think of was how too surreal this was. Having gone through all this, and still survived to become successful, made me understand why she had not given up on me. As one does while peeling open the layers of an onion bulb, Kuda had opened her life to me and was not withholding anything in the least bit. This revelation opened my understanding of a woman's worth and where her true beauty emanates from.

Having heard all this, I felt obligated to peel my own onion bulb too. Since I had left the family home, I soon found myself in shared accommodation in downtown Calgary. My world went topsy-turvy, what with being in a seven bedroomed house in a neighborhood mostly rented by University students. Without Kuda, my life would probably have gone downstream permanently. I had always taken a liking to Kuda from those high school days. Her demeanor, beauty, and exuberance had wowed me in those youthful days. Reuniting decades later was fate, I always think. After we started talking on the phone, I found her even more likeable, wise, and extremely patient with my situation. "No pressure," she would always say to me. At the same time she would set realistic goals for me to achieve within specific timelines. The irony of it was that she was being firm, although tactfully utilizing a veneer of infinite accommodation. When I look back at what she has done, I laugh at my naivety. Indeed, she would make me feel that I was in control of my situation. With a lot of encouragement and constant guidance from her, it was just in two months that I had managed to go back to work and move out of the party neighborhood.

Falling in love with a good woman is a great feeling. When all the dust was settled, and I was now back on my feet, I realized that this woman had qualities that surpassed the physical. Even though I had initially not fully appreciated the genuineness of her soul, she had given me a helping hand as another hurting human being. It started to dawn on me that I actually loved this beauty.

CANADA

Harold Sharara is an acclaimed academic, whose specialization is research in Educational Psychology, Social Sciences, and Economics. In 2005, he enrolled for graduate school and attended some of Canada's esteemed schools, including the University of Ottawa. He has a deep understanding of Quantitative and Qualitative Research Methods, and also Mixed Methodologies. He has represented different institutions at local and international conferences. Notable presentations were in Nashville TN, and Washington DC. This anthology project is his first non-academic work, motivated by what it represented for women. He felt he had to tell his story of a woman who impacted his life.

Link: http://goo.gl/eM9j4e
Link: http://goo.gl/fCVO0u

CHAPTER 23 Thobekile Mutezo

God-given Opportunities

Every one of us has opportunities for greatness, success, to better ourselves, and to serve God in a greater capacity and live the life of righteousness.

Did you know that there are dreams that come true without being dreamt about, but through God? In Jeremiah 33:3, the word of God says: *"I will show you wonderful and marvelous things that you know nothing about."* The Lord will show you marvelous things in your personal life, in your family, in your job.

Thobekile had never thought, planned, or had dreamt about relocating to the United Kingdom. Little did she know that God had something in store for her. God made it happen for her and her family. One evening, her husband came home from work and mentioned that one of his friends sent him an email about a company that was looking at recruiting people from Africa to work as surveyors in Scotland. Thobekile mulled over the idea of relocating and encouraged her husband to apply for the post to see what would happen. At the back of their minds, it was just fun. They never actually expected a response from the Company.

"If the application is successful, what are we going to do? We are settled and comfortable and happy with our lives. It's also something we have never thought about. If I got a job, what are we going to do?" he asked his wife. "If the opportunity presents itself, we will pray about it. It will be in God's hands. We don't know what he has in store for us. God is in charge of our lives. When he opens a window for you, no one can shut it," she told him. Thobekile and her husband were devout Christians.

A week after filling the on-line application, the husband got an e-mail back with the dates for the interviews in Botswana. The couple were so shocked, yet pleasantly surprised. It was time to think seriously about what they wanted to do in life. This was going to be a game changer as well as an adventure for the whole family. It was agreed that the husband went for the interview. If he got the job, it was going to change their lives. Thobekile had to support her husband; even though she was not going to be in the interview room.

On the day of the interview, the wife accompanied her husband, even though she was not going to be holding his hand in the interview room. She made sure they arrived with enough time to sit, relax, and have a coffee to settle her husband's nerves. When he went in, the wife found a quiet place and prayed hard.

"I think I have got this one in the bag," he told his wife when he came out of the interview room with a huge smile on his face. "How did it go?" she asked him. "The interview went very well," he told his wife confidently. "Thank God. I have never prayed so hard in my whole life. If you get the job, this is going to change our lives," she said.

They went back home and to their lives as usual. When they didn't hear anything for two weeks, they thought that he didn't get the job after all. It hadn't been their dream to relocate to the UK anyway.

The husband was convinced from the interview that he might get the job, therefore he needed the response regardless of the outcome. He was interested on the feedback so he could improve his skills for the next interview, etc. Now into the fourth week, the husband came from work with a bunch of papers in his hand with a big smile on his face. When Thobekile realized the smile on his face, something rang in her mind – the interview! Very curious, she asked the husband, "What is it? Tell us the good news. You look very excited and what are all those papers for? Are you working from home tonight?" A lot of questions were thrown at him at the same time, not even given the time to respond to any of them.

Thobekile's heart was now pounding very fast and she was a bit scared at the same time asking herself unanswered questions, "What is it? Is it promotion at work, or did he get the UK job? Eventually the husband handed the bundle of papers that he was carrying over to his wife and he said, "Read it for yourself." The wife received the papers without any hesitation and quickly read through, quietly, for about two minutes. Then she lifted her head up and said congrats with a big smile on her face and went on to say, "That's us going to UK. Surely God have no respect of a person. If the portion is yours, He will surely direct it to you without fail. We give all the glory to the Almighty." At this point in time, the husband was just quiet, asking himself whether to accept the offer or not. On the other hand, he was trying to weigh all the options and also looking at the advantages and disadvantages that may come with the package. He was struggling to come up with appropriate answers for all the options he was looking at and thinking about them.

The difficult part of it was that this man was a mummy's boy. Now the dilemma was, if he decided to take the offer, how was he going to cope being far away from his mum that he visited every month or even every forty night. Now thinking of being away 12,000 miles away was really a challenge. Funny enough, Thobekile was thinking the opposite of it. She kept on reading the letter through and through, smiling, pinching herself, asking herself, "Is this real or is it a dream?" She was just waiting for the husband to ask her if they were taking the offer; she had already had the answer, and never even thought twice about it as she believed that this was an opportunity from God. She had no doubt about it.

Thobekile still read through the letter time and again. These words came out of her mouth as she was still looking down on the papers, "God is real. He is faithful and just. He does not care about your background, your status, or who you are, but He opens His door for you when it is the right time and take you to another level, towards your blessing in store for you."

Remember, these people had no plans or dreamed about UK in their lives, so really an opportunity like this was unbelievable and beyond their expectations. In short, it was a miracle, indeed a revealed hidden opportunity I tell you. This was not a man-made thing, but a miracle from God. Thobekile raised her voice, giggled, and said, "Thank you Lord," and she burst in tears of joy. She continued to thank the Lord and the husband joined in and they were both in tears. We were faced with the dilemma of whether to take the job or not.

During this emotional time, the husband looked at his wife in tears and asked her, "What do we do now? Do you think we can accept this offer or just let it go since we had no plans of relocating at the moment, and again it is very far from our parents?" The wife responded very gently as she had realized that her husband was still not keen on this. If she was not careful enough, this opportunity could just go under the drain and they may never get another opportunity like this again.

With a soft loving voice, she looked at her husband right in his eyes and said, "I think we can give it a try darling and see how it goes. If it does not work for us, we can always come back." She then went on and said, "I think this is our breakthrough and I believe God has got something big for us over there in the UK. I used to hear people talking about miracles, but today a miracle is at my door step. The husband did not accept the suggestion there and then, but he said, "Okay, I heard all what you have said. But before we make any decision, let's sleep over it for a day or two, and do some research about Scotland and everything else." The wife responded with a disappointed voice, "It's actually a good idea. Let's pray about it and hear what the Lord says about it." Now at the back of her mind, she was convinced and prepared to convince her husband to take the offer and that there was no going back about it.

Three days down the line, everyone in the house was busy praying and researching on Scotland and the entire UK. They both came up with advantages and disadvantages, but agreed to compromise. The husband agreed to take the offer. The wife was very happy and continued to thank the Lord for the marvelous things that He was revealing for her family. Now it was all joys for both husband and wife and they agreed not to break the news to anyone, even to the children, until everything was in place, such as a work permit, visa, etc.

Like she said before, this was not a man-made thing, but God's appointed time. After the husband accepted the offer, everything went on very well. The work permit and visa were processed smoothly within a short space of time. This was towards the end of the year, Christmas time, and they were in Botswana. To them, it was a really good end of the year with a big breakthrough so they went home with joy.

Now after everything was in place and it was the time to break the news, the dilemma was how were they going to say this to other family members, and how were they going to take it? The husband and wife had never showed any interest of going to the UK before and now it would be, "We got the job, everything else is ready, and we will be going on such a date." It was hard for them, especially the husband, so he decided to leave everything to the wife to tell the family as she was the one who was more interested about it.

Well, the wife was fine with that. She went ahead without wasting time and told those she thought they were supposed to know and everyone was happy about it. The time came and the husband left first for the UK. Then the family followed after two months and when they arrived, their entire lives changed. Life in the UK was completely different from Africa although it was a bit stressing, but it was for the best. Now they have lived there for over a decade and they have not decided to go back to Africa at all.

When they got into the UK, they only rented a house for six months. They then managed to secure a mortgage and became landlords in a foreign land before they were able to do that back home. Remember, earlier on the wife said, "You never know, maybe God has got big things for us in the UK." Things were happening and everyone around them was amazed how their life was moving so fast, especially when they managed to secure a mortgage in less than a year. Surely God was in control and He was at work with them, revealing their hidden opportunities.

UNITED KINGDOM

Thobekile Mutezo is an Internationally Published Author, born and raised in Zimbabwe. She has worked in customer service, and has done several vocational studies including cutting & designing. She has ten years of experience in social care, working with children. She lives in Scotland with her family, and enjoys empowering her children, especially in today's world which is presented with many life challenges. Thobekile's passion for children is also partly fulfilled by being a Sunday School teacher. She is passionate in helping people achieve their goals, and this has led her to pursue a BSc (Hons.) degree in Occupational Therapy.

mutezot@yahoo.com
https://www.facebook.com/thobekile.mutezo

CHAPTER 24   Crystal Cathell

Stand By Me

I was not ready for goodbye. Mom had always been there and I didn't want to let her go. I fought against losing her, despite each harrowing loss suffered as strokes, diabetes, and dementia tore through our lives. This was different. Permanent. Final. Forever.

Nine days before Christmas, I got the call just after 7 am. Caller ID relayed what I already knew before the nurse tearfully confirmed, "Honey I'm sorry, your mom is gone." Yet, it couldn't be true. It couldn't be.

Only the night before, I'd felt renewed hope that we had more time. Breathing on her own, she'd eaten two hearty meals (after not eating more than a spoonful in weeks) and had the clarity for a good talk with the nurse. Sparkling eyes and set jaw demonstrated long absent determination I believed signified her willingness to fight for her life. We all did. In hindsight, she was ready to move on. I wasn't.

Mom never wanted to be dependent on someone for her care. Refusing to be stopped by limitations, her first stroke left her slower, a little unsteady, and less sociable, but continued to manage her apartment and daily affairs. She was the most capable woman I've ever known.

From that moment, the days tumbled by in quick secession, culminating into a few years. Everything changed so fast. Soon, her difficulties writing and remembering found me filling in her checks, paying her bills, and setting up meds. Burnt pots and pans pushed to the back of the cupboard explained the new cookware she "just felt like buying". Barely thawed chicken and broccoli she'd served for our dinner lead me to find a moldy, forgotten meal in the microwave, revealing more struggles with autonomy. Her love of driving her Mustang made it hard to believe when she gave me her keys, explaining that she'd backed into a truck and "Just can't get my foot to cooperate with my brain anymore." The birthday card with my name misspelled in a scrawl I no longer recognized caused considerable alarm I didn't know how to address. So,

I didn't. Suddenly, I was transferring from full to part-time pharmacy work to help her.

A horrific diabetic induced stroke accelerated the spiral, resulting in several broken ribs, a lengthy hospital stay, and long-term rehab in a nursing home where every visit became an exercise in agony. Before my eyes, the fight drained from her body and the fire left her spirit as the strong, capable, independent woman I'd once known seemed destined to live out the remainder of her days from the confines of a hospital bed.

I quit my job to take care of her, failing to realize it would be the hardest, most life-changing work of my life. While teetering on the brink of total dependence, she occasionally managed a small square of a sandwich, held awkwardly between fingers of a hand that no longer worked the way it used to. Attempting to find her way to her mouth, she smeared more onto her face, clothes, and hands than she ate. Clarity became exceedingly rare, glorious, and golden in her (our) darkness. Stealthily and greedily, illnesses stole away her mind and memory, and ravaged her frail body and failing spirit. With bloodthirsty determination and calculating carelessness, they left behind a broken, shriveled, unrecognizable image of the woman she used to be, taking away the very one I could not bear to lose: my mom, my friend, my confidant, my champion. She was the one who saw the best in me even when I couldn't, kicked me in the behind when necessary, and would go to the ends of the earth for me.

I had no idea how much worse it would get. Ignorance might be bliss but denial can be dangerous. Her refusal to wait for assistance getting up lead to several falls. For her safety and my sanity, I installed a bed alarm that sounded every hour or two, around the clock. Neither of us slept much – I lost track of days.

When the alarm sounded, I jumped to my feet but the heavy thud of her fall came before I even made it out of the kitchen. Soiled and disheveled, she lay crumpled on the floor. While checking her over carefully, my fear, frustration, and exhaustion mingled as I discovered I could not lift her off the floor. At wit's end, I didn't know what to do.

How I desperately wanted her to become well – to get up, walk, talk, to be healthy and whole again! Somehow, I'd managed to convince myself that mom would always be with me, but despite all my efforts and intentions, I could not save her from this. I couldn't even get her off the floor! Resentful, scared, angry, and incredibly guilty about my anger, I held her until help arrived. I was going to lose her. In many ways, I already had. And I would experience that loss countless times before the end would come.

Mom qualified for hospice care. Her original prognosis of a couple months meant she wasn't likely to make it through Christmas. At one point, I apologized for asking about something I didn't understand and was given invaluable advice: "Don't apologize for caring about your mom or asking about her support. She is your loved one. The best advocate for any loved one is always another loved one."

For weeks, mom suffered profuse vomiting and diarrhea. Repeatedly soiling herself, me, her clothing, bedding, the floor, and the portable toilet, she lost twenty pounds. I cried in the darkness as I held her hand through the night I was sure would be her last. Then, in the wee hours of morning, she attempted to speak. Many times we had stood united, facing whatever came our way. Now, she could not stand. She had lost the fight. She wanted it to be over.

She'd asked whether I'd alright if she passed on. Death was coming. Whether it be agonizingly painful and slow or immediate, it would still take her. How would I, how could I ever be alright again? Through gut wrenching sobs and blinding tears, I told her how much I loved her and never ever wanted to be without her, but would somehow find a way if she needed to go. I let her know her love, guidance, and faith inspired me to be who I am. I apologized for every hurt and disappointment I'd caused her. In the darkness of that long night, anger and frustration gave way to peace and intense thankfulness.

Mom transferred to small adult care facility with a twenty-four hour dedicated nursing staff. Her appetite increased, she spoke in short sentences, and sat with other residents. Mom was back! Hope returned. She was going to be okay!

Both the excitement and improvement were both short lived. Sometimes change, like moving, trigger responses from the brain that cause it to respond the way it used to. Patients in the last stages of life rally, often more than once, before the end. But she made it through the holidays and I was grateful. Focused gratitude, recorded in a journal, helped me survive the roller coaster ride by accentuating all I had to be grateful for, like the morning a former Beatle's song reminded me of a particularly cold winter day we'd spent thawing frozen water pipes beneath our trailer. That song had begun to play while we celebrated our success with popcorn on the stove, mugs of hot chocolate, and a handful of jaffa cakes. Mom had sang and danced me around, assuring me she would always love and stand by me. My reminiscing brought with it smiles and tears, and the need to see her. My greeting was met with silence. Not hearing her say "I love you" was the hardest part of the disconnect. And so, I talked…a lot, as I sometimes did…about anything, everything, and nothing…filling the spaces that used to include her questions, answers, her wisdom, laughter, and love. Sharing my memories, I played the song. Slightly nodding, she turned towards the music!

She's HERE! She's with me! Softly, I began to sing, growing louder as I saw the corner of her mouth turn upwards into a slight smile. Mom is smiling! I keep singing but I'm also crying. She smiles so rarely these days…and she's "with me" even less. Taking her hands in mine, I revel in the moment as we "dance", gently rocking to and fro. Overflowing with joy, tears stream down my face. Days, hours, and years slip by so fast! For a brief moment, I am seven once more and hear mom telling me to never forget how much she loves me. Hugging her, I tell her I love her and to never, ever forget that. Faint tears shine upon her face. She cannot speak but I know her love is still with me. Growing weaker and ever nearer her moment to exiting this world, she still stands by me. And I love her dearly.

A year passed and again, I'm told that mom may not make through the holidays. Throughout this, our "bonus" year, my heart has shattered countless times. Yet every time, I am reminded to remember that this is all a gift. All of it. That faith, hope, and love endure all things, even this.

I was not ready for that call. Wailing and sobbing for hours, I prayed and pleaded for it to not be true. She didn't want a memorial service but I needed to mark the moment, to honor her in some way. I felt inspired to bake her special recipe Red Velvet Cake, tied to many beautiful, magical moments with her by my side. Following suit, my daughter and I worked together, baking and bonding in our sadness and celebration. Over cake, tea, and memories, family said their formal goodbyes.

With heaviness of heart, I turned the calendar on December nearly a year later. I'd pretended this moment would not arrive. One solid year of goodbye, of letting go, of hurting and healing. I do not wallow or dwell, but I do not fight the feeling. I allow. I am in pain. I miss her. Tears keep springing up from the well…one year has come too soon. I want her here! I need her! I need her compassion, her smile, her challenge, her trust, and her truth. I need to hear her voice say, "Crystal, I love you." My heart still breaks and tears still roll. I can't stop them. I don't even try. Once, I wasn't sure I'd ever smile or laugh again. Some days are better, easier than others. But by allowing myself to hurt, I've also allowed myself to heal.

Unquestionably, mom's life shaped and moulded mine. Her illness tested it, calling on the best in me – sometimes bringing out my worst. Her death transformed it, and is still transforming it. She always managed to give me roots and wings. Even in death, she still has.

Two years have since passed. My former life burnt to the ground. As the smoke clears, I am here, beginning anew. Life is far more precious and sacred now. It's not the time we have that marks the depth of experience with our loved ones, but what we do with it. I dare not take any of it for granted – even moments of blackest night. We may be "undone" by a situation that God will use to rebuild us, stronger, better, and more alive for Him. With faith, I believe this is one of those experiences and trust God to lead the way.

UNITED STATES

Crystal Cathell makes her published writing debut with her contribution to *The Depth of Her Soul – Beautiful Stories of Faith and Empowerment*. Crystal is certified as a TEFL (Teaching English as a Second Language) instructor, Reiki Master, Personal Assistant and Home Care Assistant. She resides on the Eastern Shore of Virginia with her best friend and husband, and their very "spoiled" dog, Pepe. Currently, Crystal is creating a photography exhibit and book to celebrate the natural beauty of the Shore and serving as mixing engineer for her husband's upcoming Christian CD. Crystal volunteers as audio technician for United Christian Church of Parksley, Virginia.

Blog: http://www.mycrystalvision.org
cathellcrystal@gmail.com

CHAPTER 25   Leah Lucas

Walking Through Fire

My story is one of hardship and personal growth about how I lived in a realm of darkness in my own life and mind, but chose to turn all the negatives into positives and move forward into a better life for myself and my family.

Speaking for myself, I have never had an easy life. I was born from an amazing woman who raised me as best she could with the life she was given. My mother recently passed away, and I look to her and my grandmother every day to guide me from above the heavens. I miss them every second of everyday.

I often sit alone in my room listening to music, playing around with my favorite drum sticks, searching for answers to the many questions I have in life. None of those answers are ever directly found either. Still I sit, listening to the words of songs that have meaning to me in some way, and replay in my mind all the hard, very dark times, and challenges in my life that lead me to the place and woman I am today.

You see, I had a husband, a job, a house, a car, and a great little family at one time not so very long ago. Life should have been happy and progressing as I had always dreamt of since I was a child. I even had a dog! Things did not turn out all roses and happy for me like I had in my dreams. During my pregnancy with my son, I became very ill, and endured three emergency surgeries before my son was even born. The last operation left me with a disease that I would end up fighting for nearly six years, leaving nothing but a train wreck of heartache, sadness, and devastation behind. Not to mention a drug addiction, alcoholism, and severe depression, to name a few.

I soon found myself divorced and alone. My world was very, very dark and I saw no way out but death. I had little faith in God at this time. I blamed him for all the things that happened to me. I felt like he inflicted this awful, unfair, and unjust life on me for no reason at all. I had always grown up poor, on welfare, and watched my entire family toil day in and day out. I left my life behind and married my high school sweetheart that I had always dreamt that I would. Yet, it all came crashing down around me and I struggled to understand why. I was very angry, bitter, and placed blame on God himself for not protecting me through it all. He then took everything away from me, leaving me completely alone, feeling empty and worthless with no place to turn. Little did I know what my life was holding for me in the future.

One night in my total grief and despair, I cried to God to save me from the darkness. As I laid there shaking and crying, all of a sudden I felt warm and comforted in my bed. Like arms wrapped around me, I felt safe, warm, reassured. I stopped shaking. The tears reduced and I was able to fall asleep. I awoke the next day and got ready for my visit with a friend. Before I left, I held a knife to my wrist at the sink. I had a one-sided conversation with God at that moment and my life changed forever. I held the knife in my hand at my wrist and said, "Either you give me the strength to end my life here and now, or stand with me and show me how to get through this life, because I cannot do this on my own." Those words changed me from that point. I knew within hours that I had let go of the wheel of my own life and let God take over for me. I started my own business cleaning and organizing the homes of the people who lived in my community. I found myself going to church, and talking to people I never would have before. I went to rehab and sought counseling to be a better mother to my kids.

I was feeling better about myself and went out one night. I ended up being raped. I was found in a stairwell in the early hours of the morning crawling out of the doorway in a parking garage. The guy was never found, and I sought counseling for that also. I survived yet another tragic event that has shaped me into who I am.

I was trying my best even though I was still very much struggling every minute of every day. My divorce was final and I moved into a place I could just barely afford, but I was on my own, paying for it myself. I had said to everyone I knew that the move was the start of a new beginning for me and my kids. I was stepping forward and was scared to death, but I was happy to be on my own.

The days carried on and I fell into a dark sadness that I thought would never end. I was fighting nonstop with everyone I knew, was unhealthy, and sick. I had a total break down one weekend – when my life and that of my children and everything I knew in my entire life would all be taken away from me.

May 24th, 2014, Memorial Day weekend. The house I was renting caught fire. All I knew, all I owned, all I had worked for, even our two pets burned to nothing but ashes. In a matter of hours my entire life was destroyed and I was left homeless with nothing but the clothes that I had on, and my car. Had things gone normal that weekend for me, my children and I would have all been asleep upstairs. I can't bear to think of what could have happened had we been in the house that early Saturday morning. I let my ex-husband keep the kids that weekend because I was sick and needed a mental break. God was watching over us very closely. We all walked away with nothing but our three lives. R.I.P. to our kittens – we miss them every day.

I was forced at this time to give my two children to their father as I was left homeless and without any renters' insurance, wasn't able to recover from such a devastating loss. The Red Cross put us up in a hotel for a few days and found me some clothes to wear and some food. My church stepped in as well. So did countless others who only knew me through Facebook. I had made my profile public as to try and get the help I needed to get past this devastating event in my life.

I went through the summer staying in a few homeless shelters around Seattle and by the beginning of August, I had found a part-time job and a house share room situation. I had just moved into the house and started working, getting my life on track when things took yet another devastating turn in my world. My mother, who I have always been very close to called and told me she had stage four lung cancer. She needed me. I then packed up the only things I had in four suitcases and moved to Southern California to my sister's place and lived there for the next eight months.

After being homeless through no fault of my own, sleeping in a tent in the rain, and not knowing at times when I would even eat again, to have my mother call and tell me she was dying was just the icing on my "how could all of this be happening to me right now" cake. I was so lost, confused, and beside myself as to how I was going to cope with the loss of truly everything in my life in all literal terms of the word loss. I cried A LOT. I sat with my mother everyday watching her struggle to even breathe on some days. I witnessed her go through her battle with chemo, as sick as she was. I struggled with being present for her. I was forced to leave my kids after the fire and become homeless. I had to fight beyond measure of words to not end my life. I prayed all day and all night looking for answers as to how I was going to get through all this loss and pain; the deep never-ending sadness that I was faced with for months. I knew that I needed to be by my mother's side during her last days, and in doing so I found myself and the strength I needed to start over and because I truly had nothing left. I had a real shot at a true beginning with nothing to hold me back. My mother went through her chemo to the end.

I then packed up my bags and moved back to Washington with a family member. I worked through the summer to earn enough money to move back to Seattle and start over again. With a clear plan in mind, nothing would stand in my way this time. I was in Washington for only two weeks when I got a call that my mother had suffered a serious stroke. She passed away on March 25, 2015. I was not able to attend her celebration of life either due to work. I needed enough money to move back to my kids in Seattle at a scheduled time. I was working two jobs, doing everything I had to do for my kids' sake. I moved back to Seattle in July 2015, down the street from where my children lived with their father. I found work a month later. I have since changed jobs to a full-time office position that I love, and am now registered for school to continue with my dream of becoming a Real Estate agent in the near future.

I worked very hard to get through all the pain and loss in my life from just the last two years. I chose to look at the fire in this way: all that I held onto mostly from my past was primarily painful memories that I could not let go of, and it was killing me daily to live my life the way. I was so lost inside of myself. The fire was God's way of setting me free to move forward with a purpose. It was a way that would be happy and loving for my children and myself by showing and teaching me that through great loss and devastating tragedy, I can learn to be present in all things in life and live without anger and bitterness from all that I had endured. I had two options in my eyes. I could have let any one of those huge events take over my life and could have easily ended it all in a matter of seconds. Instead, I chose to ask God to be with me and show me the way. I dumped all the feelings in a mental barrel and chose to completely let go.

None of this was easy. I feel I have seen and endured far too much pain and loss at my young age of forty this year. However, I now live every day to inspire and be a light to others who have lost their way. Life can be very brutal sometimes. If I can only touch one person's life by sharing my stories of loss and hope, my purpose becomes clear.

What I thought was my ending truly was my beginning. For that I am now grateful.

UNITED STATES

Leah Lucas is a single mother of two amazing kids. She works for a leading Property Management company and is studying at Bellevue College for her AA in Business Management in Real Estate. Leah is an inspiration to all around her. She has fought to become who she is today after hitting rock bottom in her own life. Her smile and outgoing personality makes her great company. Her quirky humor and point of views allow her to see things from different angles. Leah is a caring, intelligent, and peace loving woman who gained wisdom through life experience. She enjoys work and her family.

Email: Lucas_Leah@hotmail.com
Leah.lucas.127@facebook.com

Conclusion

CONCLUSION

It is my wish that reading each and every story shared by these amazing co-authors, leaves the reader feeling encouraged and in some ways challenged. We all need to be tested to dig deep within ourselves and break free from feeling powerless, defeated, discouraged, undervalued, and lacking the determination to leave those relationships which no longer serve us. It could be a bad relationship with self that is causing you to make all the wrong decisions. Alternatively, it could be an association with friends who are toxic, but for some reason, one feels trapped. Each one of us is on a journey, and just like any trip, one needs a journey planner. We need to know where we are going, and also which path is risky to take. We need to understand our own compass, strengths, weaknesses, and to seek help if we feel compelled to.

Everything we require is found within us, but sometimes we need to create space for new things. When we are pushed to the limit and realize that things could not get any worse, we surprise ourselves by what we are capable of doing. There are healthy support systems and networks at our disposal. Let us use them to find our purpose sooner than later. We deserve the best!

I am now working on my second book in *THE DEPTH OF HER SOUL* series. If you are interested in becoming one of my co-authors, please contact me as soon as possible.

Email: monicasbookproject@gmail.com

Facebook: https://www.facebook.com/monica.kunzekweguta

www.ingramcontent.com/pod-product-compliance
Lightning Source LLC
Chambersburg PA
CBHW070616300426
44113CB00010B/1553